Azura & Ventura

P&O Cruises' Grand Princesses

Brian David Smith

Title page: The **Azura** *is the flagship of the P&O Cruises fleet and is caught in the bright morning sun of Dubrovnic as she arrives in the Croatian port. (Neven Jerkovi)*

Below: Seen at the Norwegian port of Stavanger in the summer of 2014, the **Azura** *is the youngest of the Grand Princess Class and is easily identifiable from her sisters by the duck tail on her stern. (Miles Cowsill).*

Ferry
Publications

Published by:
Ferry Publications, PO Box 33, Ramsey, Isle of Man IM99 4LP
Tel: +44 (0) 1624 898445   Fax: +44 (0) 1624 898449
E-mail: ferrypubs@manx.net   Website: www.ferrypubs.co.uk

Contents

Editor: Rosalind Stimpson

Produced and designed by Ferry Publications trading as Lily Publications Ltd

PO Box 33, Ramsey, Isle of Man, British Isles, IM99 4LP

Tel: +44 (0) 1624 898446   Fax: +44 (0) 1624 898449

www.ferrypubs.co.uk   e-mail: info@lilypublications.co.uk

Printed and bound by 1010 Printing, China © Lily Publications 2014

First Published: November 2014

*A very powerful view of the **Azura** as she departs her home port of Southampton on one of her popular two week cruises to the Mediterranean. (Andrew Cooke)*

Foreword

BY CHRISTOPHER EDGINGTON

The *Azura* and *Ventura* are two of the largest and most popular ships ever built for the British cruise market, and it's easy to see why these two "Grand Princesses" inspire such devotion amongst all who sail on them.

Even the hardiest of landlubbers cannot fail to be awestruck by the sheer scale and elegance of these classic ocean-going beauties the first time you stand close to them. Stepping on board is simply thrilling and it's an experience that doesn't abate over time, and isn't lessened by familiarity. I still get that same sense of excitement and anticipation every time I travel, as I'm certain many of our passengers do.

One of the great pleasures, and indeed privileges, of my position as Director of P&O Cruises, is being able to travel on the likes of the *Azura* and *Ventura* and witness our passengers having the time of their lives on board. As the largest family-friendly ships in our fleet they inspire a

sense of wonderment from the youngest children to the most seasoned of cruisers, and it's great to see all generations enjoying themselves aboard these magnificent ships.

Today, both the *Azura* and *Ventura* continue to remain amongst the most popular ships in the British cruise market, representing the pinnacle of a business we've been honing for over 175 years. Brian Smith's book offers a fascinating insight into the history of these fine ships, and the superb photography perfectly encapsulates their spirit as pioneers of the British cruise industry. I hope you enjoy it; happy reading!

Christopher Edgington
Marketing Director

Introduction

The Peninsular and Oriental Steam Navigational Company was one of Britain's leading passenger shipping companies of the 19th and 20th centuries. From humble beginnings in 1837, when the company was first formed to take the British Royal Mail to the Iberian Peninsula, it soon grew into a major player in the passenger shipping industry with large modern steam-powered ships sailing to the Orient, India and other destinations in the British Empire. Its two founders, Brodie McGhie Willcox and Arthur Anderson, were visionaries who saw that the future of world shipping was with steam-powered ships and guaranteed timetables whilst many of their competitors resisted this untested science and continued to offer passage by sail. Not only were the company credited with revolutionising the way ordinary people looked at travelling by sea, but also with persuading the Royal Navy that the future of Britain's sea defences and its place as a world power would depend on the Admiralty replacing its aging fleet of sailing ships with newer steam-powered vessels. In two World Wars and in other conflicts, most recently the Falkland Islands of 1982, P&O (as the company has always been affectionally known) has answered the call of its country and supported the military in the most exemplary fashion. Who will ever forget the television pictures of cruise ship the *Canberra* and car ferry the *Norland* in San Carlos Water right in the heat of battle, and both with a P&O crew on board!

Today the cruise ship division of the old P&O is owned by the American cruise giant Carnival Corporation and marketed as P&O Cruises. The company is, without doubt, Britain's leading cruise line with seven beautiful ships offering more destinations than any other UK cruise operator.

*An early morning arrival at Napoleon's home island of Corsica for the **Azura** means that her passengers have all day to explore the many wonderful beaches, vineyards and other exciting destinations that the island has to offer. (P&O Cruises)*

The contemporary story of the company is just as fascinating as its history. P&O's introduction of two sister ships, known as the super-liners for Britain, were the first British passenger ships to break the 1000,000 ton barrier. Their size meant that P&O Cruises were able to introduce to the British cruise market a number of innovative ideas such as outside cinemas, alfresco dining over 50 metres above the waves, cabins for single passengers, and endless swimming pools. When combining these facilities with the largest choice of bars and restaurants ever seen before on a British ship, including a restaurant by Marco Pierre White, it is evident why these two fascinating ships offer something for everyone and are without a doubt the most exciting ships that holidaymakers could ever wish to sail on.

This book explains how each ship was designed and built, and why both have developed such a large number of dedicated passengers who love sailing on them. Beautifully illustrated with photographs from respected marine photographers as well as P&O's own heritage collection, and including some intriguing photographs provided by their builders, Fincantieri, this book will be a welcome collection to both the maritime enthusiast as well as the many people who want a fabulous souvenir of their holiday on one of these two wonderful cruise ships.

Brian D Smith,
November 2014

Azura & Ventura

The History of P&O Cruises

Today, P&O cruises is a very successful British company owning seven ships, all dedicated to the British cruise market and sailing to various locations around the world. They have a proud and interesting history which can be traced back to the early 19th century when in 1815 Brodie McGhie Willcox started trading as a shipbroker in a small office, close to the River Thames in the centre of London. Not a great deal is known about how well Willcox did in these early years, but he clearly traded with some success as in 1822 he had the need to employ a young clerk from the Shetland Islands by the name of Arthur Anderson who had served with the Royal Navy during the Napoleonic Wars and therefore had some important maritime experience to add to the company. Such was Anderson's drive and enthusiasm that within three years of joining the company, Willcox decided to make him a partner and in 1825 the two of them started trading as Willcox and Anderson. Not only

finished than a further civil war broke out in Spain. Again, Willcox and Anderson sided with the legitimate Queen and once again backed the winning side. This was to be of great importance to the company in later years as the Spanish Ambassador to London would use great influence to help the company win new contracts to the Iberian Peninsular.

SAIL GIVES WAY TO STEAM

At this time there were a number of great and famous men who were starting shipping companies using steamships, including Isambard Kingdom Brunel who was running a single ship service across the Atlantic to New York with his latest ground breaking vessel, the *Great Western*. The problem was that steamships were still in their infancy and were extremely unreliable. When ships broke down there was, more often than not, nothing to replace them and Anderson quickly realised that for a shipping company to succeed it needed to

An oil painting by T.F. Dicksee showing P&O's co-founder and Chairman Arthur Anderson in 1850. (Ferry Publications Library)

Brodie McGhie Willcox, also painted by T.F. Dicksee in 1850. (Ferry Publications Library)

Captain Richard Bourne, owner of the William Fawcett, who collaborated with Anderson and Willcox in creating P&O. (Ferry Publications Library)

did they act as shipbrokers, they actually became ship owners after a small American schooner had gone aground near Dover and her owners had wanted to sell the wreck to limit the liability of the damaged ship. Once Willcox and Anderson had purchased the vessel, they repaired her and fitted her with some defensive armaments before sending her on her first journey for the company to Portugal carrying various cargos and a small number of passengers. The name of this ship is not known but it began a dynasty that continues today in the form of P&O Cruises.

During this period Portugal was involved in a civil war and Anderson began the very dangerous and risky business of gun running for the Portuguese Crown and its supporters, which included an elderly British Admiral by the name of Sir Charles Napier who later worked for Anderson. The decision proved to be a wise one as the Queen of Portugal won her war and rewarded Willcox and Anderson with contracts to serve her country from the UK. No sooner had the war in Portugal

have a fleet of vessels which included a spare ship ready to enter service if required. In 1834 they decided to rebrand their company with an eye to making it the premier company taking cargo and passengers to the Iberian Peninsular. A prospectus was issued with the company name of The Peninsular Steam Navigation Company, the Oriental suffix was added later when they began to explore routes into the Mediterranean and across to Egypt.

In 1835, the Spanish Ambassador in London took steps to introduce the benefits of a reliable steamship service to Spain and chartered several steamships from the Dublin & London Steam Packet Company. He did not forget the involvement of Willcox and Anderson in supporting the Spanish Queen a few years before and so placed the management of this new venture under the Peninsular Steam Navigation Company.

To supplement this additional trade, the company purchased a 206-ton paddle steamer called the *William Fawcett* which had been built in Liverpool in 1828. With two large sails and twin paddle wheels, she had been named after the engineer who had built her engines and is regarded as being the first ship actually owned by the Peninsular Steam Navigation Company. To give some idea of comparisons, the *William Fawcett* was less than 100 metres long and her engines had a total output of around 60 horse power. P&O Cruises' latest ship, the *Azura*, is almost 300 metres long, 120,000 gross tons, and her engines have a total power output closer to 100,000 horsepower.

By 1837 Willcox and Anderson owned a fleet of seven steamships which were all fitted with auxiliary sails whilst most ships at this time were sail ships with auxiliary steam engines. They had many competitors who were struggling to make their steamships pay, but Anderson believed that if they could offer a regular service which would leave exactly when advertised and arrive at its destination at a designated time

Above: In 1835 the **William Fawcett** *was charted to open services to Spain and Portugal. (Ferry Publications Library)*

Right: A lithograph by J.I. Herdman depicting the Mediterranean service liner the **Great Liverpool**, *ex* **Liverpool**, *as she appeared in 1840. (Ferry Publications Library)*

then people would be willing to pay the extra needed to make the service viable. It is important to remember that at this time, most services were dependent on the wind and tide, and timetables were little more than a planner's dream. With the strong currents in the English Channel and the heavy seas off the Bay of Biscay it could take anything up to 10 days for a ship to reach Portugal from London and on occasions even three weeks could be the norm.

A TIMETABLED SERVICE

Clearly matters had to improve and Anderson realised that if he could reduce these times and provide a reliable service then his new company was in with a chance of success. It was decided to advertise a sailing from Falmouth to Vigo in Spain that would take only 54 hours, an unbelievably

quick time for the period. There would be a sailing connection to London which would take another two days but they were offering a real timetable from England to Spain which was significantly shorter than any other company could ever hope to offer. Willcox was still worried about making such a business profitable, but Anderson convinced him that if they could win another large contract delivering goods to the continent then the business would be a success. The suggestion came from Richard Bourne, one of the company's senior employees who had joined them in 1835 from the Dublin & London Steam Packet Company, that the way to make their new company profitable was to win the Royal Mail contract to Spain and Portugal. He believed that any company that took the Royal Mail across the sea always made a profit. The current contract to run the mail was up for renewal so Willcox immediately put plans together, ready to tender the Admiralty when the contract was advertised. After many deliberations between the three executive figures of the Peninsular Steam Navigation Company, they managed to offer the Admiralty a fixed timetabled service for which they would charge the Government £30,000 per annum to take the Royal Mail to the Iberian Peninsular.

The Admiralty were reluctant to do business with the three men but Willcox, by now an MP, managed to convince

the Government that they could do the job safely and reliably.

No one else could match the price or delivery times that Willcox and Anderson were offering so on 22nd August 1837, the new contract to carry the Royal Mail to Iberia was duly signed. This is now regarded as the official beginning of the company which today trades as P&O Cruises. On 1st September, the largest ship in the fleet, the 450-ton *Don Juan* left England bound for Spain carrying the first cargo belonging to the Royal Mail and on board were Anderson and his wife Mary Ann. The operation with the Royal Mail was so successful that within a year the Government asked the company to make plans for taking the mail from Gibraltar right through to Alexandria in Egypt. The importance of winning this contract could not be underestimated as the significance of Alexandria was not simply the mail or the trade

route to Egypt itself, but the fact it was the next staging post for the lucrative mail run to India and countries beyond the subcontinent.

TO THE ORIENT

The Suez Canal, linking the Mediterranean to the Red Sea, was still some time from being completed by the French, and it was not until 1869 that it was open for traffic. In the 1830s it involved ships docking at Alexandria or Cairo before their passengers and cargo continued their journey across the Isthmus of Suez, a slow and sometimes dangerous desert journey of 150 miles on camel or donkey. One of the reasons that the British Government gave the Alexandria contract to the Peninsular Steam Navigation Company was that they promised to send the mail in modern steamers calling at British ports such as Gibraltar and Malta on the way. Others sent the mail partly across land and France in particular. There was never any evidence that the French authorities interfered with the British Mail but Britain had been at war with France for as long as anyone could remember and there were many members of the British Government who were not yet ready to trust the French with the British Royal Mail.

To take on this extra work the company needed additional ships and employees, but before it could do this it required incorporation by Royal Charter which would grant the company Limited status. It finally received this in December 1840 alongside a new set of directors with Willcox and Anderson remaining as Managing Directors. The name Oriental was officially added to the company's name and from this point on it was known as the Peninsular and Oriental Steam Navigation Company or, more affectionately as P&O for short. In exchange for shares, the company acquired a ship from a trans-Atlantic company who had run into difficulties after one of its competitors, Samuel Cunard, had won the Atlantic Royal Mail contract. It is interesting to see that Richard Bourne was completely right in his prediction that any company that won the contract to carry the Royal Mail had a greater chance of success as today, be it in a significantly different form, the only two significant shipping companies that were trading in the 1830s and still survive in the 21st century are P&O Cruises and Cunard; both of whom had Royal Mail contracts from the British Government.

In the 1840s, the only company taking the Royal Mail to India was the powerful East India Company whose Royal Charter went right back to the times of Queen Elizabeth I. They controlled all the mail from Bombay to the UK and were not about to give up this very lucrative trade without a fight.

The terms of P&O's charter were that it could take the mail to India but it did not state what part of India. Rather than cause friction with a registered heavy weight company with influential friends, P&O decided to send the Royal Mail to Calcutta. The problem with this was that most passengers wanted to go Bombay and not Calcutta and had been used to extremely lavish ships offering a great deal of comfort; albeit

that they were still powered by sail and very slow. To compete, P&O were going to have to build at least two new and very large, comfortable steam ships that were capable of taking a combination of passengers and cargo to run between Suez and India. By running a steamship service so far from home, P&O were coming up against a set of logistics that had never been encountered before.

In those days it was not just a question of fuelling and storing in England and then setting sail and arriving in India a few weeks later, as there were no established places to take on additional coal and provisions. Sailing ships carrying coal had to be dispatched in advance to various locations on the route to await the steamer where it would then refuel. The sailing ships would also carry agents to these locations where they would arrange to purchase fresh water, food and other provisions.

The new ships would cost £60,000 each and would be wooden paddle steamers of around 2,000 tons with a length of 240 feet. Each would have 60 cabins and berths for 150 people. They were elegant ships with three masts of sail and two funnels. They had clipper bows and wide stern windows. The normal arrangement for passenger ships of the time was to have the public rooms in the centre of the ship with the cabins at the forward and after ends. P&O decided to reverse this with large passenger rooms at the bow and stern and the cabins running in the middle of the ship, the idea being that in rough weather the centre of the ship tends to move around less and therefore when people were resting in their cabins they would have a more comfortable passage.

The first of the new ships, the *Hindonstan*, sailed from Southampton for India on 24th September 1842 via Gibraltar, St Vincent, Ascension Island, Cape Town, Mauritius and Ceylon taking a total of 91 days. Upon her arrival she immediately set sail for Suez on what was to be her regular route via Madras, Ceylon and Aden. The second ship was named the *Bentinck* and joined her sister in the following year. P&O could now take the Royal Mail and passengers from London to India using the *Great Liverpool* or the *Oriental* from England to Alexandria before everyone went across land to Suez where they would pick up one of the new ships on to India. The journey times were significantly shorter than those being offered by the East India Company who could still take up to a year to reach India, going around the Cape of Good Hope in South Africa.

GROWING THE PASSENGER TRADE

After winning the new mail contracts to India, Willcox and Anderson looked at new ways to increase the profitability of their company without the need for any additional expenditure. Anderson managed to convince Willcox that people would be willing to pay good money to travel on their steamships and to visit the many interesting ports and countries that P&O traded with. It was another imaginative idea which he had originally conceived back in 1835 when he ran a small newspaper in the Shetland Isles called the

Top: The **Poonah** *at anchor in the Grand Canal at Venice, the first large steamer ever to visit the city. (Ferry Publications Library)*

Above: In this 1875 etching from The Graphic, the captain of P&O's **Sumatra** *is leading a Sunday religious service on deck as the steamer progresses through the Red Sea. (Ferry Publications Library)*

Right: The **Himalaya** *built in 1892 was the second ship in the fleet to carry this prestigious name. (Ferry Publications Library)*

'Shetland Journal'. In one particular issue there was empty advertising space which Anderson had been very keen to fill up by any means necessary. So he used it to advertise 'Ghost' cruises on local ships plying the waters around the Shetland Islands that didn't even exist.

However, it was not until 1844 that the first ever real cruise was advertised in the British press, sailing from England to the Mediterranean and such exotic destinations as Malta, Athens and Rhodes.

The novelist William Makepeace Thackery was given a complimentary ticket by P&O on one of their first ever cruises as a way of obtaining free advertising for the new venture. He wrote the book 'Notes of a Journey from Cornhill to Grand Cairo' under the pseudonym of Michael Angelo Titmarsh and travelled on several ships, including the *Lady Mary Wood*, the *Tagus* and the *Iberia* to Gibraltar, Greece and Egypt, all of which were scheduled services rather than a leisurely cruise to those destinations. Thackery was very grateful to P&O for their kindness and wrote very highly of them, if not the places that he visited, but the strategy worked and P&O had their free publicity. P&O's network of Mediterranean and Black Sea routes continued to build in the 1840s, including a route to Constantinople. However, these were not as successful as the routes to India and the east so some of them were dropped in favour of the more lucrative Royal Mail services.

The start of the Crimean War in 1853 put a stop to any cruise trade that P&O had built-up in the Mediterranean, and although the war lasted less than 30 months, it was some considerable time before cruising was again considered by the company. In the meantime they continued to expand their services throughout the Indian Ocean and the Far East, although this rapid expansion of ships and routes was to have its problems. For one thing the amount of coal which needed transporting to the ports where P&O ships were refueling increased significantly. Every steamship on a trip to India needed three sailing colliers to sail ahead of it, making sure that there was enough coal for the ship to arrive at its destination. It was estimated that at any one time P&O had over 90,000 tons of coal stored around the world ready for their ships to use on its routes to and from Britain. P&O also had to feed up to 10,000 people per day at a time when there was no frozen food or refrigeration. Ships were going to sea with entire farmyards on board, all of which would have been eaten by the time the ship arrived at its destination. To help solve this problem P&O began building its own farms on land close to the ports were the ships refueled. This way less livestock needed to be put on the ships in Britain, meaning there was more room to carry additional cargo and a plentiful supply of suitable meat was always available once the ship had sailed.

Other shipping companies were very jealous of the success of P&O and a parliamentary enquiry into the company was held in 1852. This found no wrong doing by the Board of Directors and upon its completion the company celebrated its findings by winning the Royal Mail contract to Australia. The East India Company could not compete with the new and expanding company and its services to India were deteriorating as they desperately tried to hang on to their mail contracts to Bombay. They were now vastly inferior to P&O when it came to reliability, timings and comfort.

In response, the East India Company subcontracted some of its work carrying the Royal Mail and did so to less than reputable companies who on occasions lost the mail in transit. To obtain the Royal Mail run between London and Bombay it had secured subsides from both the Indian and British Governments to the tune of over £105,000 a year at a time when P&O were waiting for the chance to out-manoeuvre the ailing company and take its trade. The opportunity came after a gross act of complacency when the East India Company managed to lose an entire consignment of Royal Mail after it had arrived at Aden where there were none of the company ships to take it on to Bombay.

Rather than wait for one of their ships to arrive, the company decided to send it on to India in an Arab dhow which left Aden and was never seen again. Upon receiving news of this debacle, the P&O board immediately submitted to the British Government a set of proposals promising to deliver the Royal Mail to India using only its large modern steamers, stopping at only British controlled ports and for a subsidy of only one fifth of what the Government had been

paying to the East India Company. The fate of the East India Company was sealed and P&O finally won the profitable Royal Mail run to Bombay.

Matters were progressing well for P&O and the future was looking very bright when the original founder of the company, Brodie McGhie Willcox died in a freak accident just outside Portsmouth in 1862. The co-founder and driving force Arthur Anderson died a few years later in 1868. At the time of their deaths the Peninsular and Oriental Steam Navigational Company had 51 steamships in service, more than any other shipping operator, and had expanded from a simple service to the Iberian Peninsular to a large multi-national company serving the British Government and carrying hundreds of thousands of passengers to three continents. In 31 short years P&O had become one of the largest and most successful shipping companies the world had ever seen.

UNDER NEW LEADERSHIP

Anderson's choice for his successor as Chairman of P&O was a young Aberdonian called Thomas Southerland. He had joined the company when he was 18 and served at various levels on most of their trade routes. He had shown a drive and determination similar to that of Anderson himself and quickly demonstrated that he was a suitable replacement for the great man when he managed to open a new trade link to Japan, at a time when only the Dutch had been allowed to do business with what was then still a very closed and secret country. He returned to work at the company's headquarters in London, and in 1872 was voted as P&O's new Managing Director at the very young age of only 38 years.

The Suez Canal had finally opened in 1869. This caused P&O a few problems, as new tonnage had to be built for the now direct service to India. The Government wanted to renegotiate its subsidiary for taking the Royal Mail as now it could be done much more efficiently and cheaply. As a result P&O saw its revenues drop at a time when its expenditures were rising; the opening of the Suez Canal was not a happy event for P&O's finances. However, the company persevered and by remaining true to its principles of offering large modern, comfortable ships, with a quick and reliable timetable, it soon overcame these adversities. This was best demonstrated in 1887 when Queen Victoria celebrated her Golden Jubilee and P&O marked the occasion by building four 6,000-ton 'Jubilee' ships, the *Victoria*, the *Britannia*, the *Oceania* and the *Arcadia*.

The company was able to make this patriotic gesture because of its success in meeting the challenge that the opening of the Suez Canal had presented. The jubilee ships had three-cylinder, triple expansion steam engines producing 7,000 horsepower and turning a single propeller giving them a top speed of 16.5 knots. They had a length of 466 feet and a beam of 52 feet. Each ship cost £188,000 and was placed on the company's top links to India and Australia. The first two were built on the River Clyde by Caird & Company whilst the second two were built by Harland & Wolff in Belfast. All could carry 250 First Class and 159 Second Class passengers.

The ships were not fast like their counterparts on the North Atlantic but were broader in the beam and more comfortable in rough seas. The livery that was now adopted by P&O was a black hull, buff deck housing and black masts and funnels. The crews were generally made up of Indians in the engine-room, Lascars (Indian sailors) on deck and stewards from the Portuguese colony of Goa. It has been suggested that the term 'POSH' originated from this time when influential passengers travelling to India had their tickets stamped P.O.S.H, indicating that their cabins were to be located on the portside outwards and the starboard side on the way home, thus benefiting from being on the cooler side of the ship in the afternoon whilst travelling in both directions.

THE CRUISING MARKET

By this time, the nature of P&O's trade had altered radically as revenues from the Royal Mail contracts were diminishing whilst those from passengers and cargo were increasing. In the space of 20 years the size of the fleet had increased from 80,000 tons to 200,000 tons and the run to Bombay had been reduced in time by more than a week. P&O was Britain's premier shipping company serving the Far East and very much an Imperial institution. It still had close ties with the British and Indian Governments allowing its vessels to be chartered for such uses as hospital ships and troop transports when the need was necessary. The company was doing well yet still wanted to explore ways of generating new revenue streams. It was about this time that Arthur Anderson's idea of using P&O vessels for cruising was reconsidered as, by this time, other shipping companies were beginning to advertise their own particular cruise ship services. This included the North of Scotland, Orkney and Shetland Company who began cruising to the Norwegian Fjords in 1886 and the Orient Line which started cruising to the Mediterranean and Scandinavia in 1889. Both of these companies had found success at an early stage and quickly turned this new industry into a handsome profit for their owners. This did not go unnoticed by P&O who would later acquire both companies. Their success gave P&O the impetus to purchase a 23-year old ship called the *Rome* and convert her into the company's first ever real cruise ship in 1904. Built by Caird & Company in 1881, the *Rome* was just over 5,000 gross tons and her steam engines could provide around 850 horsepower giving her a top speed of around 12 knots. Renamed the *Vectis* she was more of a luxury yacht for the rich and famous rather than a cruise ship for the masses but she served the company well for eight years before being sold to the French Government in 1912.

One thing P&O had not planned for was the sudden expansion in cheap immigration travel which simply exploded at the start of the 20th century. Much has been written about this phenomenon, especially the two most famous companies plying this trade across the North Atlantic: the White Star Company and the Cunard Line. Their ships had grown in size

and speed in two completely different ways with one going for speed over comfort and the other going for comfort over speed. This cumulated in the ultra fast *Mauretania*, *Lusitania* and *Aquitania* being built for Cunard and the ultra luxurious *Olympic*, *Titanic* and *Britannic* being built for White Star; but for P&O the story was rather different. Up until 1910 they had concentrated all their efforts on the Royal Mail runs and the passage of wealthy First Class passengers, which is why there was no Third Class on their 'Jubilee' class of ships. In 1910, P&O decided to take over the Blue Anchor Line which was a well known family-run business sailing between Britain and Australia, around South Africa, taking emigrants and cargo on the outbound journey and tea and wool on the return.

It had traded well in small, efficient, if sparsely appointed vessels until 1909 when the company was struck by disaster as their newest and largest vessel, the *Waratah* disappeared without trace on a voyage back to the UK with the loss of all 211 people. The company never fully recovered from this disaster and the takeover by P&O in the following year was welcomed by many of the old employees of the Blue Anchor Line who felt that as part of the P&O empire they had a greater chance of holding onto their jobs and a more prosperous future. With the acquisition of the Blue Anchor Line, P&O could now trade at both ends of the passenger market with First class passengers travelling to India and Australia via Suez and Third class passengers going via the Cape.

P&O GOES TO WAR

As for Thomas Sutherland, he had now been with P&O for almost 60 years and was very close to retirement. In 1914 two major events took place that were to shape the future of P&O. Firstly, P&O merged with the British India Company allowing Sutherland to retire and for the British India's Chairman, Lord Inchcape, to take control. Secondly, the Great War started with over 100 ships from the P&O group of companies being requisitioned by the Admiralty for military service. Within 24 hours of war being declared P&O's first requisitioning took place when the *Himalaya* was ordered to Hong Kong for fitting out with eight 4.7 inch guns. She became an armed merchant cruiser protecting trade and shipping in the China Sea. In Britain two further P&O ships, the *Mantua* and the *Macedonia* were also similarly converted and this was all in the first week of the war. Convoys started to leave India to support the British Expeditionary Force in France with over 30,000 Indian troops being moved in one convoy alone.

Considering the amount of tonnage that was lost during the Great War (around 15,000 ships sunk in total) P&O came out of it relatively unscathed. Their worst loss occurred on 30th December 1915 when the 7,974 gross tons *Persia* was torpedoed in the Mediterranean near Crete. Nearly 500 feet long and with a beam of 53 feet, the *Persia* was powered by the highly advanced, triple expansion steam engines capable of driving the ship at over 18 knots. She was attacked by U boat

*P&O **Medina** leaving Portsmouth in 1911, carrying King George V and Queen Mary to India. (Oil Painting by W.Wyllie)*

U38 at around midday whilst most of the passengers were having lunch, killing 343 of the 519 people on board. The ship had gone down with a huge fortune of gold and gems belonging to the Indian Maharaja Jagatjit Singh who had fortunately not been on the ship at the time of the sinking.

The proudest moment for P&O during the war was when Captain Archibald Smith of the *Otaki* was posthumously awarded the Victoria Cross after his ship engaged the German surface raider *Moewe*. As a civilian, Captain Smith was not entitled to be awarded the Victoria Cross, and his exploits were kept secret as it was viewed that military recognition of the defence of his ship would affect treatment of merchant prisoners of war.

The last ship lost by P&O during the conflict was the *Suranda* which was torpedoed on 2nd November, just nine days before the Armistice. In all P&O lost around 500,000 tons of shipping throughout the Great War but due to the increase in ship building capability, managed to finish it with roughly the same amount of tonnage that it had started with.

FLEET EXPANSION

At the end of the war there was a strong rumour that P&O was about to purchase Cunard when in fact they finally bought the Orient Line and the Khedivial Mail Line. This was in addition to the Union Steamship Company which was bought in the last full year of the war. P&O's requisitions did not stop there, with the General Steam Navigation Company being purchased in 1920 and Strick Line in 1923. Of the 300-plus German civilian ships that had been seized by the British Government at the end of the war, P&O bought 98 of them as passenger traffic rose sharply after the end of hostilities.

A company milestone was reached in 1923 when the *Mooltan* and the *Maloja* became the first ships ordered by P&O to be over 20,000 gross tons. A second company milestone was reached in 1924 when for the first time ever P&O recorded a profit of over £1 million. This allowed the company to go on a major spending spree where the four famous 'C' class ships were introduced. The *Cathay*, the *Comorin*, the *Chitral* and the *Corfu* were all over 15,000 tons and were powered by two four-cylinder quadruple expansion steam engines, each powering its own propeller and giving a service speed of around 16 Knots. They were 547 feet long and over 70 feet wide and could carry 203 First Class and 103 Second Class passengers on the company's premier service to India and Australia. All four ships were built by Barclay Curle & Company on the River Clyde with the first two being launched on the same day by Lord Inchcape's wife and daughter.

It did not stop there, with the larger and equally famous 'R' class following on with the *Rajputana*, the *Ranchi*, the *Ranpura* and the *Rawalpindi*. These were improved versions of the 'C' class and could take 307 First Class and 288 Second Class passengers. All of the 'R' class were built at the lesser known Harland & Wolff shipyard of Greenock in Scotland, and upon entry into service were placed on the prestigious run to Bombay.

P&O's most famous ship of this time was the Royal Mail Steamship the *Viceroy of India* which entered service in 1929. Originally ordered in April 1927 under the name *Taj Mahal* she was just under 20,000 tons and built by Alexander Stephen & Sons on the Clyde. She was appropriately launched on 15th September 1928 by Dorothy, Countess of Halifax, the wife of the then Viceroy of India. The 'Viceroy' was revolutionary in that she was only the third vessel in the world at that time to have turbo-electric machinery rather than steam expansion engines for her propulsion. Compared with other passenger ships in the P&O fleet at that time, the *Viceroy of India* was a fast ship, having a service speed of 19 knots which allowed her to break the London to Bombay record with a time of 16 days 1 hour 42 minutes soon after entering service in September 1932. The accommodation aboard the *Viceroy of India* was truly astounding for a ship of her size, with much of it being designed by Elsie MacKay, the daughter of the P&O Chairman. She was the first P&O ship to have an indoor swimming pool and the first to have individual cabins for all of her First Class passengers. The quality of her appointments was not restricted to the higher grade passengers alone. P&O had designed the interiors of this ground breaking vessel so that comparable advances were made in the level of comfort enjoyed by all classes throughout the ship. She was the last P&O ship to be built with the traditional black hull and black funnels, for Lord Inchcape decided to paint the hulls of his next and final order of ships gleaming white with buff funnels. This was to be applied to all new P&O ships from this moment forward and is a policy that continues to this day.

This last order of Inchcape's was for five ships which were to become known as the White Sisters or the 'Straths' after the lead unit, the *Strathnaver*. She was launched on 5th February 1931 at Vickers Armstrong Ltd of Barrow in Furness

by Lady Janet Bailey, second daughter of the P&O Chairman. This new ship was big by P&O's standards but much smaller than the liners on the crack North Atlantic run which by now had reached over 80,000 tons in size. The new ship was 639 feet long and 80 feet wide. She had a total gross tonnage of 22,547 tons and could carry 498 First Class passengers and 670 Tourist Class passengers, as Second Class were now to be known. She sailed on her maiden voyage from London on 2nd October 1931 to Australia via Marseilles, Suez, Bombay and Colombo. The second ship was the *Strathaird* and followed her sister into service a year later in 1932. This was a very sad year for the P&O Group as it lost its charismatic and popular Chairman, when Lord Inchcape suddenly died.

DEPRESSION AND ANOTHER WAR

Lord Inchcape had been rewarded by the British Government for P&O's contribution to the war effort of 1914-1918 and the subsequent drive to get the British economy moving with an Earldom back in 1929.

He remained in charge of P&O until his death by which time the company was starting to feel the effects of the great depression and passenger numbers were dropping. The amount of cargo being carried had been reduced significantly and even the Royal Mail contracts could not generate the huge profits the company had seen during the previous decade.

The Chairmanship of P&O fell to Inchcape's son-in-law, the Right Honorable Lord Craigmyle who guided the company through the financial strains of the 1930's where the company forced its staff to take a 10% pay cut and, more often than not, did not pay out any dividends to its shareholders. Despite this downturn in passenger numbers the company decided to continue with its order for the White Sisters and in 1935 Vickers Shipyard delivered the *Strathmore*,

*The **Strathmore** is seen in the fitting-out basin at Barrow in Furness with Orient Line's **Orion** being completed to the rear. Note that the **Orion** is painted in the old Orient Line black livery and not as delivered with a corn hull and buff funnel. (Barrow Museum)*

*Top left: The Australia Room on the **Himalaya**. (Barrow Museum)*

*Tope right: A four-berth cabin on the **Chusan**. (Barrow Museum)*

*Left: The **Chusan**'s promenade deck, showing the large windows and patio doors which could be opened on tropical evenings. (Barrow Museum)*

*Above: The launch of the **Chusan** at Barrow-in-Furness on 28th June 1949. (Barrow Museum)*

closely followed by the *Stratheden*. Both were slightly larger than the first two sisters and were instantly recognisable as they only had one funnel compared to the three of the first two ships. The fifth and final sister was the *Strathallan* which entered service in 1938 and was the last P&O ship to enter service before the outbreak of World War II. On delivery of this last ship, Lord Craigmyle retired due to ill health.

At the outbreak of hostilities, the P&O group had a total of 368 ships and just as in the First World War the company was to make a significant contribution to the British war effort. By the end of September 1939, all of the 'R' class were under Royal Navy control including the *Rawalpindi* which was requisitioned by the Admiralty on 26th August 1939 and converted to an armed merchant cruiser by the addition of eight 6 inch guns and two 3 inch guns. She was set to work from October 1939 in the Northern Patrol covering the area around Iceland. While patrolling north of the Faroe Islands on 23rd November 1939, she investigated a possible enemy sighting, only to find that she had encountered two of the most powerful German warships, the battleships *Scharnhorst* and *Gneisenau* which were conducting a sweep between Iceland and the Faroes. The *Rawalpindi* was able to signal the German ships' location back to the Home Fleet in Scapa Flow. Despite being hopelessly outgunned, the ship's 60-year old Captain, Edward Kennedy (the father of broadcaster and author Ludovic Kennedy), decided to fight, rather than surrender as demanded by the Germans. He was heard to say, "We'll fight them both, they'll sink us, and that will be that." The German warships sank the *Rawalpindi* within 14 minutes but not before she managed to score at hit on *Scharnhorst*. A total of 238 men died when the *Rawalpindi* sank, including Captain Kennedy and 54 of the 65 P&O men still on board. Some 37 men were rescued by the German ships and a further 11 were picked up by another P&O ship, HMS *Chitral*. Captain Kennedy was posthumously Mentioned in Dispatches when clearly a Distinguished Service Order or even the Victoria Cross would have been more suitable. The Prime Minster, Neville Chamberlain, told the House of Commons, "They had no thought of surrender. They fought their guns until they could be fought no more. Their example will be an inspiration to those who come after them".

The loss of the *Rawalpindi* so early in the war was P&O's worst shipping disaster in the whole conflict. Other ships were lost including the *Viceroy of India* which was torpedoed on 11th November 1942 off Oran and the *Cathay* just moments later. In one operation to launch a head on the North African coast P&O lost over 110,000 tonnes of shipping including the almost new *Strathallan*. From the invasions of Italy to D Day and the Normandy Landings, P&O ships were in support of the Royal Navy as either troop carriers, armoured cruise vessels or as hospital ships. They continued to support the British war effort right up to the end of hostilities in 1945 by which time they had lost 182 ships with a combined tonnage of over one million tonnes and over 1,000 serving crew members

The Second World War had taken a great toll on P&O but everyone knew that it could have been much worse.

AIR TRAVEL PROVIDES COMPETITION

P&O's headquarters in Leadenhall Street, London, had miraculously survived the Blitz so on Wednesday 18th December 1946 the company held its first post-war Annual General Meeting. The company was now led by Sir William Currie and he outlined the future plans by stating that passenger traffic would be concentrated on the Australia, India and China runs whilst more emphasis would be placed on its cargo business. He acknowledged that air travel would become a major player in the travel industry and that P&O should embrace this new technology and work with it rather than against it. He wanted to build new ships that were cost effective and economical to run. The company ordered its first new passenger ship, the *Himalaya* which, at cost of £3 million, was the company's most expensive ship by some distance. The *Himalaya* was built by Vickers Armstrong in Barrow In Furness and had a gross tonnage of 27,955. She was also very fast

with a top speed of 25 knots which would cut the UK to Bombay passage by five days and reduced the overall voyage to Australia from 38 days to just 28 days. By the time she entered service with P&O in 1949 much of the company's profile had changed and the number of cargo ships outnumbered the passenger ships by three to one.

The decline in passenger numbers meant that as older tonnage was sold off or scrapped, it was not necessarily replaced as the number of passenger ships leaving P&O far exceeded the number being built. A mere total of six new ships were built for P&O from the end of World War II to the start of the 1960s including the *Chusan* of 1950 and the second *Arcadia* in 1954. A smaller version of the *Himalaya*, the *Chusan* had a tonnage of approximately 24,215 gross tonnes and a capacity of just under 1,000 passengers. She was built by Vickers Armstrong in Barrow as a direct replacement for the *Viceroy of India* and was approximately 646 feet long and 85 feet wide. She was launched on 28th June 1949 and christened by the wife of Viscount Bruce of Melbourne, entering service on 1st July 1950. The new ship was extremely luxurious and well received by both her passengers and crew. One of the reasons for this was that the *Chusan* was the first passenger ship to be fitted with anti-roll stabilizers which brought a new level of comfort to her passengers that had never been experienced before. No doubt it was a result of the *Chusan's* sea-keeping qualities that she was chosen to go on P&O's first world cruise in April 1954. The *Chusan* was also the first P&O ship to visit Japan after the end of World War II when she visited Yokohama in November 1950. She also closed the company's scheduled services to India when in January 1970 she left Southampton for the final time on a direct sailing to Bombay.

The second *Arcadia* was built by John Brown shipyards on the Clyde and was launched on the 14th May 1953. She was slightly larger than the *Chusan* at 29,734 gross tonnes and served on the Australia run for her entire career until she was retired in 1970. Both the *Chusan* and the *Iberia* undertook many cruises from London and Southampton to the Mediterranean and other more exotic destinations such as Asia and South America.

Such was the success of the new jet airliner that passenger numbers continued to dwindle and in the middle of the 1950's P&O were to order the last two ships which were to serve on any of their companies scheduled services. In what was a gloomy period for the company, no one ever envisaged that they would go on to have such long and successful careers and that one of them would become one of Britain's most famous and best loved ships of all time. In 1955 it was announced that two new large and extremely fast passenger ships would be delivered for the Australia service in 1960. The first would go to Orient Lines and would be called the *Oriana* whilst the second would be for P&O and in reference to the company's strong ties with Australia, would be called the *Canberra*.

*The Clyde-built **Arcadia** in the English Channel in the early 1970s, by which time her rear mast had been removed. (FotoFlite)*

NEW SHIPS FOR A NEW AGE

On 3rd November 1959, HRH Princess Alexandra launched the *Oriana* at the Vickers Armstrong shipyard at Barrow In Furness. She was the last ship ever built for the Orient Line as the company was fully absorbed into P&O operations in 1966 giving the corporation a new name of P&O Orient Lines. As a result, when she entered service she still wore the Orient Line traditional colour scheme of a corn-coloured hull with white superstructure and corn-coloured funnels. Her maiden voyage was from Southampton to Sydney in December 1960 and at 41,915 gross tonnes and a capacity for 2,000 passengers in two classes (First and Tourist), the *Oriana* was briefly the largest passenger liner in service on the UK to Australia and New Zealand route, until the introduction of the *Canberra* in May 1961. The *Canberra* had been launched by Dame Pattie Menzies, wife of the Australian Prime Minister Robert Menzies, at Harland & Wolff on the 16th March 1960. She was the last passenger liner ever to be built at the famous Belfast shipyard which could pride itself on the construction of some of the biggest and most famous passenger ships of all time.

The *Canberra* was the most technically advanced ship built by P&O since the *Viceroy of India* back in 1929. All of her engineering spaces, and subsequently her funnels, were placed at the after end allowing vast open areas in the middle of the ship to be developed as passenger areas. She was the first P&O ship to be fitted with bow thrusters to assist maneuvering and had a real cinema on board as well as full air conditioning throughout. Arguably the single most remarkable feature of the *Canberra's* design was her turbo-electric propulsion system. Instead of being mechanically coupled to her propeller shafts, the *Canberra's* steam turbines drove large electric alternators which provided power to electric motors which, in turn, drove the vessel's twin propellers. They were the most powerful steam turbo-electric units ever installed in a passenger ship with around 42,500 horsepower per shaft.

All of today's modern cruise ships are powered in a similar fashion with large diesel engines replacing the *Canberra's* steam turbines. As if this was not enough, the *Canberra* also had another feature which made her unique and set the standard for all of today's large cruise ships. Her lifeboats were placed three decks lower than usual for ships of her type and were recessed into the hull to allow improved views from the passenger decks. This was not only much safer for the passengers as in an emergency the boats did not have to be lowered right from the top of the ship, but it also allowed for a huge amount of open deck space to be made available to the passengers. This proved an immediate success for her mainly British passengers who had an unrivaled love of being outside when at sea.

Once the *Canberra* had entered service some of the older ships in the fleet were retired and P&O settled down with a fleet of just over 20 ships, of which most were of reasonably modern tonnage. By the mid 1960s air transport had killed off all of the trans- Atlantic passenger traffic and was now eating into the Australian routes as well. P&O's profits were hit hard and the new chairman, Donald Forsyth Anderson, had to make some very difficult decisions which involved selling and laying-off ships, and of course cutting the number of people that they employed on their services. Despite the ongoing problems of the Suez Canal and the occasional mishap, including the *Oriana* colliding with an American aircraft carrier and the *Canberra* catching fire, the two ships became firm favourites of the company and were much loved by their loyal passengers.

*The **Spirit of London** arriving at Southampton during her early career with P&O. (FotoFlite)*

By the start of the 1970s things were not looking too good for the company and they began to dispose of all their ships which were not making a profit or did not have a future with the company. The *Chusan*, the *Orcades* and the *Iberia* were all scrapped in the Far East, and the *Himalaya*, the *Orsova* and the *Oronsay* soon followed, leaving the *Oriana*, the *Arcadia* and the *Canberra* as the mainstay of P&O. The solution to their long term futures was to turn these ships into one-class cruise ships and for P&O to concentrate on the holiday market as a way of returning these giants back into profitability. The P&O board saw a great future in this area of leisure, especially in the North American market where cruising was far more popular, no doubt due to the year-round hot weather in the Caribbean and the fact that the average American had more disposable income than his European counterpart. This persuaded the board to buy the successful American company of Princess Cruises in 1974, and from this point onwards the cruising arm of the P&O Group was to be known as P&O Princess Cruises.

With their change to cruising, the *Oriana* and the *Canberra* settled back into a regular routine, which would see them both based in Southampton and operating two and three week summer cruises. The *Oriana* would spend the winter months based in Sydney with the *Arcadia* whilst the *Canberra* would start the New Year with a three-month world cruise. In 1977, the Chairman of P&O announced that the passenger division had made a £4.1 million profit in the previous trading year as opposed to a loss of £6.9 million in 1975. In 1979 the decision was taken to scrap the *Arcadia* as she was seen as being too old and outdated for any future use with the company, her place in Sydney was taken by the *Oriana* leaving the *Canberra* as P&O's sole ship sailing out of Southampton.

P&O AND THE FALKLANDS CONFLICT

On 1st April 1982, Argentinian forces invaded the British Falkland Islands and thus began a conflict which was going to have serious repercussions for all British merchant shipping. At the time, the *Canberra* was at the end of her world cruise and heading through the Mediterranean back to the UK. Captain Dennis Scott-Masson received a message asking for his estimated time of arrival at Gibraltar, which was something of a surprise to him as it was not on the ship's itinerary. When he called at Gibraltar, he learnt that the Ministry of Defence had requisitioned the *Canberra* so that they could use her as a troop ship and he was to immediately sail to Southampton. Other ships in the P&O fleet that were requisitioned included the educational cruise ship *Uganda*, the two ferries *Norland* and *Elk*, the tanker *Anco Charger* and a general cargo ship called the *Strathewe*.

In all 860 crew members would remain on P&O's ships and sail to the South Atlantic with the hastily assembled 'Falklands Task Force'. After returning to Southampton the *Canberra* was modified from her cruising role into a ship more suited to her military role and sailed for the South Atlantic on 9th April, four days after the main task force, led by HMS *Hermes* and HMS *Invincible,* had left Portsmouth. On board the *Canberra* were units of the Parachute Regiment and Royal Marines who were going to take part in the landings to retake the Islands. The Cunard ship *Queen Elizabeth 2* was also requisitioned but it was decided that she was too much of a national icon to be sent into a war zone which meant that the *Canberra* was going to have to do most of the dangerous work and be sent right into the heart of the conflict.

Operation Sutton was the codename for the amphibious

assault to reclaim the Falkland Islands and as part of that assault the *Canberrra* anchored close to San Carlos Sound just after midnight on 21st May. She went forward at around 05:20 that morning unloading her troops throughout the day and under constant attack from Argentinian aircraft. The air attacks on the ships in San Carlos Water continued until 16:00, after which time HMS *Ardent* had been sunk and HMS *Argonaut* damaged. At 19:00, the order was given to disembark the remaining troops from the *Canberra*, and at 22:42 she weighed anchor and headed out of San Carlos Water and North Falkland Sound. The *Canberra* had landed around 2,000 troops and without sustaining any real damage during the day's events. She then sailed back to Ascension Island where she picked up another set of troops from the *Queen Elizabeth 2* before sailing back to San Carlos Water and again off-loading her troops in the thick of the battle. She then waited off the Islands until she was ordered back into San Carlos Sound for a third time on 15th June, this time to repatriate captured Argentinian solders back to South America.

Following the Argentinian surrender, the *Canberra* and the *Norland* took around 6,000 prisoners of war back to South America and after 94 days at sea, the Great White Whale, as the military had affectionately named the *Canberra*, returned to Southampton in what was without doubt one of the most spectacular and emotional homecomings the city had ever seen. Her Captain was awarded a CBE and made an Aide-de-Camp to Her Majesty The Queen; a very fitting tribute indeed.

After her return to civilian life and a lengthy refit, the *Canberra* returned to cruising with P&O Princess Cruises. Her role in the Falklands War made her very popular with the British public and many of her cruises were sold out months in advance. She was now Britain's most famous cruise ship and P&O started to think that the conditions were right for the company to consider ordering a brand new cruise ship, the first since the Canberra herself had entered service back in 1961. Before any new ship could be discussed, P&O celebrated their 150th anniversary with a lavish celebration on 7th July 1987 on board the Princess Cruises ship, *Pacific Princess* which had been moored up in Greenwich, London just for this special occasion. The highlight of the evening was a Gala dinner, of which Her Majesty the Queen and the Duke of Edinburgh were the guests of honour.

Once all the euphoria of the 150th celebrations had calmed down, P&O put together a team under the name of Project Gemini to work on the new ship, and after much consultation a new 69,000 gross tonnes cruise ship called the *Oriana* was ordered from the German shipyard of Meyer Werft in 1991.

ENTER THE NEW ORIANA

Delivered in April 1995, the new ship was named by Her Majesty the Queen in Southampton and upon entering service immediately became the largest and most expensive ship that P&O had ever owned. She was an outstanding success as demand outstripped supply with all of her cruises

fully booked months in advance. When the *Canberra* was compared to the new ship it was clear that she was outdated in so many ways that it would be impossible to bring her up to the same standards. The fact that the *Canberra* was a much more fuel-thirsty vessel was the final nail in the coffin and in late 1996 it was announced that the most popular cruise ship the company had ever owned would be withdrawn from service. Her final cruise left Southampton on 10th September 1997 for a 20 night cruise around the Mediterranean, during which she met up with the new *Oriana* in Cannes where passengers were able to go across in tenders for a visit on P&O's latest flagship. Later the same day, the 'Golden Cockerel', a large metal silhouette of a cockerel on a pole traditionally carried by the fastest ship in the fleet, was handed over to the *Oriana* in a ceremony eagerly watched by passengers of both ships. Upon her return to Southampton the ship de-stored before heading to Pakistani ship breakers where it took over a year to dismantle one of the last passenger ships ever built in the UK.

To replace the *Canberra* it was decided another brand new ship was to be ordered from Meyer Werft which would be even bigger than the *Oriana,* and to transfer the *Star Princess* from Princess Cruises to P&O where she would become the third ship to be called the *Arcadia*. As the British cruise market continued to grow it was also decided to transfer the *Sea Princess* which would become the *Victoria* giving P&O three ships until the arrival of their new vessel after the millennium. The new ship was named *Aurora* on 27th April 2000 by Princess Anne at a lavish ceremony in Southampton before setting off on her maiden voyage on 1st May. Regrettably this was aborted after just a few hours when a stem tube bearing overheated and failed causing the ship to return to Southampton before heading back to Germany for emergency repairs. She finally entered service later that month with a 10-night cruise to the Canary Islands.

P&O PRINCESS CRUISES PLC AND CARNIVAL

Just before the *Aurora* entered service it was announced that all cruise ship operations were to be de-merged from the P&O group, forming a new independent company which would be known as P&O Princess Cruises PLC. This new company would also operate the other passenger shipping companies now owned by P&O including the German cruise company Aida Cruises, the river cruise company, A'Rosa Cruises and Ocean Village Cruises, a new company which was aimed at the younger and less formal market. The whole company would become independent of the P&O Group but would remain under the control of P&O's latest Chairman, Lord Sterling of Plaistow.

In April 2003 P&O Princess Cruises PLC was bought out by the American Cruise Company, Carnival Corporation, after an initial offer from rivals Royal Caribbean Cruise Lines was turned down by the P&O Board. This made Carnival the world's biggest cruise operator with more cruise ships than

*The **Canberra** shows her graceful lines as she speeds through the English Channel. (FotoFlite)*

any other company. Apart from Carnival Cruises itself the company also owned Holland America Line, the Italian cruise company, Costa Cruises as well as Cunard which it purchased from Trafalgar House in 1998, meaning that the two giants of British shipping were now owned and operated by the same American company.

As soon as Carnival had completed the purchase of P&O Princess Cruises it split the company into its own individual brands which would all be controlled by the parent company from the US. This meant that P&O would now be branded as P&O Cruises with its own head office in the UK and its own set of directors which would steer the company into the 21st Century.

The success of the *Oriana* and the *Aurora* was assured with record numbers of people now sailing from the UK on P&O Cruises' ships. The demand was increasing at such a significant rate that Carnival took the bold decision to transfer two of Princess Cruises' new 'Sun' class ships to P&O Cruises, which at around 77,000 tonnes were similar in size and capacity to the *Aurora*. Known as 'The White Sister', the *Ocean Princess* and the *Sea Princess* became the *Oceana* and the *Adonia* and the two vessels were renamed together in Southampton on 21st May 2003 by Princess Anne and her daughter Zara Phillips, the first double ship naming ceremony in history.

Carnival's plans for the expansion of P&O Cruises did not stop there, with an announcement that they were to get a brand new ship which for the third time in less than ten years would be the biggest and most expensive ship the company had ever owned. One of the advantages of belonging to Carnival was that it brought with it a wealth of talent in cruise ship design and operation such as with the Holland America Line who, since their acquisition by Carnival, had three new

ships built which were collectively known as the 'Vista' class. The 'Vista' class was a Panamax (Panama Canal maximum size) design of ship with a tonnage of around 85,000 tons and room for just over 2,000 passengers on a hull design that had a smooth and modern appearance. As the third ship in the P&O fleet to be called *Arcadia* had been transferred to Ocean Village Cruises, it was decided that the new ship would become the fourth *Arcadia*. She was launched on 26th June 2004 and entered service with the company the following April. Upon the entry into service of the *Arcadia*, the *Adonia* was transferred back to Princess Cruises and reverted back to her original name whilst a smaller Princess Cruises ship, the *Royal Princess*, was transferred to P&O Cruises and renamed the *Artemis*.

The success of P&O Cruises continued to grow as passenger numbers sailing out of Southampton continued to grow at a substantial rate. In the last year of the 20th Century fewer than 300,000 people were cruising from the Port of Southampton but, by the end of the *Arcadia's* first year in service, this number had more than doubled to over 700,000 and the number was still rising. Carnival saw the potential growth and decided that as Britain's most popular cruise line, P&O Cruises were in a good position to take advantage of this expansion. Therefore, in 2006, they announced that the company was to receive the next ship of their 'Grand' class design, which up until now had been exclusively for Princess Cruises, meaning that for the first time ever P&O would have a ship of over the magic 100,000 tonnes mark.

THE 'GRAND' VENTURA AND AZURA

The 'Grand' class started life in 1997 when the *Grand Princess* entered service and briefly became the world's biggest ever cruise ship. The *Ventura*, as the new ship was to

*The **Oriana** inward bound to Southampton. (FotoFlite)*

Top: The **Aurora** *at the start of her River Ems passage to the North Sea. Just like the* **Oriana** *thousands of people turned out to see the giant ship leave the shipyard. (Meyer Werft*

Above: The **Ocean Princess** *was one of four white sisters built for Princess Cruises before being transferred to P&O Cruises in 2002 and renamed the* **Oceana**. *(P&O Cruises)*

Right: The **Adonia** *was originally the eighth of a series of sister ships built for Raddison Cruises around the turn of the century. She joined P&O Cruises in April 2011 and is currently the smallest ship in the fleet. (P&O Cruises)*

be known, was the tenth ship of this design and again was slightly modified from her sisters to suit the requirements of both P&O Cruises and the British cruise market. The keel was laid on 26th August 2006 and launched less than a year later. She was named by Dame Helen Mirren on 16th April 2008 before departing on her maiden voyage to the Mediterranean two days later. Even before the Ventura had entered service it was confirmed by P&O Cruises that the final unit of the 'Grand' class of ships was going to be assigned to them, and that for the second time in two years P&O Cruises would be receiving another ship of over 100,000 tonnes. To be built at the same Italian shipyard of Monfalcone as her sister, the keel of the Azura was laid down on 27th October 2008 and

launched on the 26th June 2009 before being handed over to P&O Cruises on 1st April 2010. She was named in Southampton on 10th April by her Godmother, Darcey Bussell, a former principal dancer of the Royal Ballet. Whereas the Ventura had been principally designed for families with a great emphasis on children's facilities, the Azura was designed to appeal more to P&O Cruises traditional client base with many of the company's familiar features (including a bar named after one of its founders) making a welcome return.

The Azura is as contemporary as she is large with a number of firsts for P&O Cruises, the most obvious being the open air cinema screen on the Lido Deck and the cabin accommodation for single people. She is truly worthy of being

*The disparity between the **Azura** and the yachts in Southampton Water could not be more apparent as she glides past Netley and where the liners of the Great War used to bring the wounded home. (Andrew Cooke)*

*Top: The seven Captains from the seven P&O cruises ships raise their caps to the **Azura**'s Godmother, Darcey Bussell, as the company celebrates it's 175th anniversary. (Mike O Dwyer)*

*Above: P&O Cruises Commodore, Stephen Burgoine, leads the **Adonia** at the head of the fleet out into the Solent on what must have been the wettest July day in history. (P&O Cruises)*

*Right: The Princess Royal, Princess Anne takes the salute from the Trinity House Vessel, **Patricia**. (Mike O Dwyer)*

called P&O Cruises flagship and a fantastic testament to the foresight of Brodie McGee Willcox and Arthur Anderson. Not even they could imagine that from their humble beginnings in a small London office such a huge and impressive cruise ship, capable of carrying over 3,000 people around the world, would one day carry the name of a P&O Cruises flagship.

A GRAND EVENT CELEBRATES 175 YEARS.

On Tuesday 3rd July 2012, P&O Cruises celebrated their 175th Anniversary on what was the wettest July day in living memory. The celebrations, which were over two years in the planning, started at around 4am when the first of the company's seven ships started to arrive in their home port. The *Ventura* was on the Mayflower berth with the *Arcadia* and the *Aurora* immediately in front of her. The *Oriana* was on the City Terminal with the *Azura* on the Ocean Terminal. This left

the *Adonia* and the *Oceana* to fight for the last of the spaces on the old QE2 berth at dock head. Never before had seven cruise ships berthed together in any British port with a combined tonnage of 569,000 gross tonnes. A logistical nightmare then took place as over 30,000 passengers disembarked or embarked bringing an estimated £17 Million to the economy of Southampton.

The dancer, and new judge of the popular BBC programme Strictly Come Dancing, Darcey Bussell, who named the *Azura* back in April 2010, met the seven Captains of the seven ships on the stern of the P&O flagship before unveiling a special plaque to commemorate the occasion in Carnival House.

Later, Her Royal Highness, the Princess Royal, was the guest of honour at a special reception on board the *Oriana* where senior P&O executives such as their Managing Director, Carol Marlow, and David Dingle, the CEO of Carnival UK were joined by a list of celebrities who have an involvement with P&O such as Marco Pierre White, Atul Kochhar and Olly Smith. Also present was the life president of P&O Cruises, Lord Sterling. They all enjoyed a sumptuous luncheon which included a special cake baked by celebrity patissier Eric Lanlard.

The weather did not let up and regrettably, the evening display by the Red Arrows aeronautical display team had to be cancelled. At 17:15 the *Adonia*, under command of the P&O Commodore, Steve Burgoine, slipped her moorings and headed to the top of Southampton water where she turned and slowly started her journey out into the Solent. As she passed each of the other P&O ships they in turn left their berths and started the precession down towards the open sea. As each passed dock head, a short firework display took place as they slowly lined up for a fleet review. After the

Adonia came the *Ventura*, followed by the *Arcadia*, the *Aurora*, the *Oriana*, the *Azura* and the *Oceana*.

Once in formation the ships were due to be reviewed by Princess Anne who would be waiting for them off Fishbourne, aboard the Trinity House Vessel, the *Patricia*, with Lord Sterling, Carol Marlow and David Dingle also on board. Close by was the Royal Navy's newest ship, the Type 45 destroyer, *HMS Dragon*. To the starboard side of the ship passed the *Adonia*, the *Arcadia*, the *Oriana* and the *Oceana* whilst to the port side passed the *Ventura*, the *Aurora* and the *Azura*. Once past the *Patricia* the ships all went their separate ways on their Grand Event Cruises to the Mediterranean, the Baltic, the Norwegian Fjords and the Canary Islands.

P&O Cruises has come of age with its current fleet of seven wonderful ships, including the recently introduced *Adonia* in April 2011, each with its own unique style and ambience designed to offer something for everyone in their quest for the perfect holiday. In 2013, almost one million people cruised with P&O Cruises on a range of cruises from a two night party cruise to Belgium to a full world cruise lasting over 100 nights.

With the announcement that in 2015, the *Britannia*, an even larger and more impressive ship is to join the fleet, with even more new and innovative ideas to help people enjoy their time on board, it is clear that today's management have the same drive and dedication as their predecessors by investing and diversifying in an attempt to meet the challenges of running a successful cruise company in the 21st Century. They are without a doubt Britain's favourite cruise company, respected and admired throughout the world for their heritage and levels of service that are simply second to none.

Long may they continue to be so!

*In March 2015 the second ship to be called the **Britannia** will enter service for P&O Cruises nearly 128 years after the original. (P&O Cruises)*

VENTURA

HAMILTON

Azura & Ventura

Design & Constructio

There are many superlatives that have been used to describe P&O Cruises' flagship, the *Azura* and her sister, the *Ventura* including; "the Superliners for Britain" and "the largest ships ever built for the British cruise market". True as these informative expressions may be, the fact remains that there are a lot more to these beautifully designed ships than eloquent sound bites. Admittedly, to the purists they may not have the desired graceful appearance of the famous trans-Atlantic liners of the 1930's which are still held by many as a romantic notion of what a ship should look like, and compared with the Compagnie Générale Transatlantique's the *Normandie*, they may have a point. But what they do offer are magnificent state of the art facilities that are a necessity for a 21st century passenger ship to be a success. Not only have these Superliners raised the bar when it comes to the standards set for modern day British cruising, but these highly innovative ships have also opened up the opportunity for a cruise holiday to a large number of people who have never sailed on a cruise ship before. As the only British cruise ships over the magic 100,000 tonne mark, their size and dynamics are on a different scale to everything else, offering passengers the most varied and exciting contemporary cruise experience.

CARNIVAL CORPORATION ENTER THE BRITISH CRUISE MARKET

The catalyst for the *Azura* and the *Ventura* started back in April 2003 when the American cruise giant Carnival Corporation bought out what was P&O Princess Cruises and demerged the two companies into separate enterties under the Carnival umbrella. Carnival already owned several other European cruise companies including Cunard Line, Holland America Line and Costa Cruises which meant that they had a very large and dynamic portfolio from which it could draw on a wealth of ideas and experience, and then distribute them throughout its various corporate brands. What Carnival also brought to P&O Cruises was its powerful negotiating position with the world's leading shipyards. This gave the company a vastly improved bargaining position when it came to price and delivery for any future new cruise ship. Before Carnival, P&O Cruises had not been in a position to order more than one ship at a time for over half a century, but as Carnival normally ordered several new ships at a time P&O Cruises suddenly found themselves in a good position to receive one of a number of new ships that the parent company currently had under order at that time. This is best exemplified by the *Arcadia* which was ordered by Carnival as a ship for its Holland America Line brand, but before construction started she was transferred to Cunard Line as the *Queen Victoria*. As construction progressed it became apparent that she was going to be too small for Cunard's requirements so, for the second time in her short life, Hull 6078 was transferred to another owner and became P&O Cruises' current *Arcadia*.

The other big contributing factor which allowed the decision to bring such large passenger ships to P&O Cruises was the continued rise in popularity of cruise holidays from the UK. This was especially true of the number of families who were now choosing to spend their annual holiday on a cruise ship, and as the two previous vessels that P&O Cruises had recently introduced, the aforementioned *Arcadia* and the *Artemis*, were exclusively for adults, the other three ships in the fleet, the *Oriana*, the *Aurora* and the *Oceana* were struggling to cope with the demand for family holidays, in particular at peak times in the school holidays. With passenger numbers displaying double digit percentage increases year on year and predicted future cruise numbers showing strong growth, it was clear that to maintain their position as Britain's favourite cruise company P&O Cruises were going to need a ship, possibly two, which would be considerably larger than anything currently in their fleet and would be both innovative and appealing in their design to satisfy the needs of their regular customers as well as the many new people predicted to take a cruise holiday sometime in the near future.

THE LARGEST SHIPS EVER BUILT FOR P&O CRUISES

Under the name of Project Canberra, a team led by the head of Carnival UK's new ship building team, Stuart Hawkins, was assembled to see what unit of the Carnival Brand would be best suited to P&O Cruises and how the ship could be developed to appeal to the clientele that would be expected to use her. The team had several requirements to consider before coming to their decision. The ship had to be large enough to cope with the future projected growth of the British cruise market and offer a cabin configuration that allowed for a wide range of prices but were improved in terms of size, facilities and storage space with a majority of them having their own private balcony. There had to be a greater variety of public rooms than were currently available on other P&O Cruises ships, with a particular emphasis on children's facilities and fine dining with several alternative places to eat other than in the main restaurants. The ship needed to have excellent sports and fitness facilities with a good sized well-being area and several swimming pools, including one with a retractable roof. In other words, the new ship had to be designed for purpose, with rooms that were both luxurious and contemporary with every detail meticulously crafted to give the British holiday maker a remarkable cruise experience. From a technical point of view the ship needed to be able to carry enough fuel and provisions to cross the Atlantic Ocean and be fast enough to undertake a typical Mediterranean cruise within two weeks. She needed to have a reasonably shallow draft to allow her to visit as many different ports as was possible and to comply with not only the United Kingdom's stringent environmental regulations, but also that of the various other countries she would be visiting. She also had to be easily adaptable to suit future changes in the Safety of Life at Sea (SOLAS) regulations which are frequently updated.

It was immediately apparent that there were two types of

The two giant overhead cranes of Fincantieri combine to lift part of the **Ventura**'s *stern into the building dock. (Fincantieri)*

With precision craftsmanship, the centre block of the **Ventura**'s *bow is lowered onto the ship's hull. (Fincantieri)*

ship in the Carnival portfolio that suited the requirements for Project Canberra. The first was the Grand Class of ship that was currently serving exclusively with Princess Cruises, whilst the second was the Conquest Class which was serving with Costa Cruises and Carnival Cruises. Both fitted the design specification for Project Canberra and both had proven to be very popular with their respective lines passengers. After a series of discussions within the team and senior P&O Cruises and Carnival executives, it was decided that the Grand Class of ship would be best suited to P&O Cruises requirements as the general arrangement of these ships was already similar to that of other P&O Cruises ships and it would be the easiest to modify to suit the taste of the British passenger. It also had larger cabins which made the design more suitable for the longer voyage type that the ship would be undertaking.

A GRAND CLASS OF SHIP

The Grand Class started life back in 1994 when Princess Cruises placed an order with the Italian shipbuilder of Fincantieri for a 109,000-tonne cruise ship that was of a completely revolutionary design, with more balconied cabins than any previous cruise ship and a distinct stern lounge which sat nearly 50 metres above the sea. Built at a cost of $450 million, the *Grand Princess* was laid down as yard number 5956 at the company's Monfalcone shipyard in Northern Italy where she was launched on the 20th May 1998. She was christened in on the 29th September 1998 by the actress Olivia De Havilland becoming the worlds largest and most expensive passenger ship ever built. Two sisters of the *Grand Princess* followed; the *Golden Princess* in 2000 and the *Star Princess* in 2001.

Princess Cruises then ordered two slightly modified sisters which were to be known as the Gem Class called the *Diamond Princess* and the *Sapphire Princess* from the Japanese shipbuilder of Mitsubishi Heavy Industries in Nagasaki. The two Gem class of ship are based primarily on the Grand Class but, owing to a slight increase in the hulls width, were larger units at 115,875 tonnes. Other modifications included the placement of the stern nightclub to just aft of the funnel and gas turbine propulsion for the main engines. The contract for

the two ships was signed on the 25th February 2000 with the *Diamond Princess* being the lead ship due to be delivered in July 2003 and the *Sapphire Princess* following a few months behind with a delivery date of May 2004. On the 1st October 2002, a fire started in the art gallery of the *Diamond Princess* which quickly spread to the rest of the ship causing extensive damage to over 40% of the hull. Luckily no one was injured during the incident and none of the important engineering spaces were affected. Eventually it was decided to swap the names on the two ships and to concentrate all work on the new *Diamond Princess* so that her completion would be as close as possible to the contractually agreed date. Eventually the new *Diamond Princess* was handed over to Princess Cruises on the 26th February 2004 followed by the *Sapphire Princess* on the 27th May following a herculean effort by the shipyard to get her damaged hull repaired and completed on time.

In between the arrival of the *Diamond Princess* and the *Sapphire Princess*, Princess Cruises had taken delivery of the fifth unit of the class when the *Caribbean Princess*, which was being built back in Monfalcone by Fincantieri, entered service on the 4th April 2004. Due to continued efficiencies and progressive technical improvements in ship construction by the Italian firm, the *Caribbean Princess* had an additional deck

The three tunnels for the **Ventura**'s *bow thrusters are clearly visible as another piece of the jigsaw puzzle is carefully added to the superstructure. (Fincantieri)*

*A late evening shot depicts a shipyard welder working on one of **Ventura**'s stern blocks with her propeller mountings clearly visible. (Fincantieri)*

included in her construction which allowed for an additional 255 cabins, corresponding to an increase in her passenger capacity by about 20% to 3080 passengers, and raising her gross tonnage to 113,000 tonnes. This was mainly possible by reducing the weight on the hull by constructing the top passenger decks out of light alloy instead of steal thereby allowing the additional deck to be added without any reduction in stability or performance.

The final three of the Grand Class were to be known as the Crown Class and were all built by Fincantieri. As well as featuring the additional deck of cabins, the famed Skywalkers night club was positioned behind the funnel as on the Gem Class but the general arrangement was that of the original Grand Class. The first of the class was the *Crown Princess* which was handed over to Princess Cruises on the 27th May 2006, followed by the *Emerald Princess* on the 24th March 2007, and finally the *Ruby Princess* on the 21st October 2008.

AN ITALIAN DESIGNER

Once it had been decided that the next ship in the Grand Class was going to be assigned to P&O Cruises, a team of interior designers had to be appointed to make sure that the new ship would not be a simple extension to the previous units that had all been designed for the American cruise market, but would be quintessentially British in both appearance and character. The renowned maritime architect

Giacomo Mortola was chosen as coordinating architect as he had a proven pedigree in ship building and had worked on the QE2 as well as most of the previous Grand Class ships. As is customary with P&O Cruises, more than one team of architects would be working on the new ship, and the two British companies, SMC Design and Design Team, were chosen as well as the German firm of PartnerShip Design. Over the next few months the team set about designing the new interiors that would be both contemporary and luxurious and would be attractive to a large section of the travelling British public. As Fincantieri had built six of the last Grand Class ships, they were always going to be favorites to build the new ship, especially considering that parent company, Carnival Corporation, had ordered over 30 new cruise ships from its yards since 1995. Officially known as Societa Finanziaria Cantieri Nvali Fincantieri, the company was established in 1959 as a state-backed amalgamation of most of Italy's shipyards.

The contract for the new ship, which still had no name at this time, was signed on the 23rd September 2004 when Carnival placed an order with the company for five new cruise ships in a $2.6 billion order including the new *Queen Victoria* for Cunard, the *Emerald Princess* for Princess cruises, the *Carnival Freedom* for Carnival Cruise Lines and the *Costa Serena* for Costa Cruises. Whilst the other British ship, the *Queen Victoria*, would be built at Fincantieri's Marghera yard.

*A view from one of Fincantieri's overhead cranes shows the **Azura** at an early stage of her construction. (Mike O Dwyer)*

*The **Ventura**'s Block 16 weighs 400 tonnes and waits on the quayside to be lifted into the building dock as the late evening light deepens over the Adriatic. (Mike O Dwyer)*

*Here we see a block containing the **Ventura**'s stern cabins being lifted onto the superstructure as the familiar outline of the superliner become apparent. (Fincantieri)*

P&O Cruises' hull number 6132 would be built at Fincantieri's Monfalcone yard on the Adriatic north-west, close to near the Slovenian boarder where all the other Grand Class ships had been built.

MODEL TESTING AND HYDRODYNAMICS

The design of cruise ships has changed dramatically over the last 20 years or so and the Grand Class in many ways was the first ship of the modern design where a majority of the passenger cabins were moved from inside the hull to the upper superstructure, allowing for a large number of private balconies to be added. Normally, before any construction of a new ship takes place, a model of the ship is made and tested in large experimental water tanks where strong winds and heavy seas are simulated to see how the hull behaves in extreme weather conditions. Model testing is crucial to decipher the optimum design of a ship's hull which has the minimum resistance for the desired cruising speed. Although hydrodynamics are able to calculate the frictional resistance of a hull through water on today's modern computers, the resistance created by the wave-making of the hull can only be confirmed by extensive testing. Once this is complete the model is then subjected to various aerodynamic tests in a wind tunnel where the test on the dispersal of exhaust gages from the funnel and the affect of air turbulence over the ship are recorded and modifications made if necessary. However, as the new ship was to be a continuance of the Crown Class all the data recorded when the models for the *Crown Princess* were tested would be used on P&O Cruises' new ship, except

for some additional wind tunnel tests that were needed on the new funnel arrangement. The shape of the funnel used onboard passenger ships are formed in characteristic shapes depending on the cruise operator and the series of the ship it is based on. The funnel has to be designed so that exhaust gas from the engines do not come into contact with the open deck, the superstructure or the air intakes, while making the most use of the appearance design intended by the ship owner. Fincantieri made every effort to optimize the shape of the funnel to promote the rise of smoke emissions upwards out of the ship through a collective arrangement of multiple exhaust pipes whilst keeping the decorative structures around the funnel very similar to that of the rest of the Grand Class

Towards the front of the ship another block containing the mini suites is being lowered into place. (Fincantieri)

*The top of the **Azura**'s bow is lifted into the air as she is taken from the paint shops to the building dock. (Fincantieri)*

*Work is now at an advanced stage on the **Ventura**'s hull with most of her heavy machinery such as the engines and generators now covered with the superstructure. (Mike O Dwyer)*

The bulbous bow has to be made very smooth if it is to perform at optimum efficiency and reduce the ship's drag through the water. (Fincantieri)

fleet, but with subtle modifications to suit the P&O Cruises brand.

Once all the plans for the new ship had been completed and approved by P&O Cruises the steel needed to construct the ship had to be ordered. Fincantieri order their steel from various steel works across Europe which is delivered by sea direct to the yard in the form of large steel sheets measuring anything between 5mm and 24mm thick. Each is encrypted with an alphanumeric punched code that determines where and when it will be used during the construction stage. The type of steel used in a cruise ship is extremely strong and durable yet it has the capability to stretch when pressure is applied to it so that it does not tear, or worse fail, when it comes into contact with a heavy object. To make sure that steel used in the construction process is of a suitable quality, P&O Cruises and the shipyard have representatives, who in conjunction with the ships classification society, monitor Fincantieri's work during all stages of the construction to make sure it is up to the standard required to gain a certificate of seaworthiness at its completion.

THE STEEL IS CUT

Back in the UK, several meetings took place to decide what name the new ship should have. Eventually it was decided the new ship would be called the *Ventura* after the small American town close to the headquarters of Princess Cruises in California. Once the ship had a name, and the steel to build her had been delivered to the yard, it was time for the physical task of actually building the ship to begin. On the 29th August 2006, a small ceremony was held at the Monfalcone shipyard to commemorate the start of the steel cutting for the *Ventura*. This is the date that is recorded as the official start date for the construction process. Like all modern passenger ships, she was to be built to the modular block construction method. This involves steel being formed into large separately numbered blocks which are then lowered into the building dock and welded together. At the beginning of the process giant electronic magnetic cranes lift the steel sheets into the Preparation Shop where they are cleaned and painted with shop primer which is a type of undercoat

designed to protect the steel throughout the production process. After, it is moved to the Fabrication Shop where it is laid in a shallow pool of water where a computerised plasma-cutting machine cuts the steel to a pre-arranged shape. The reason it is cut underwater is because temperatures of up to 25,000 degrees centigrade are generated during the cutting procedure, and this way the heat generated during the cutting procedure is quickly dissipated avoiding a buckling effect on the edges. Huge pressing machines bend the steel sheets into the required form using nothing more that wooden moulds before they are moved to the welding shops for assembly into small panels which are around 50 tonnes in size. These sections are then given additional strength by the addition of transverse and longitudinal stiffeners known as beams and girders which are attached to the ships frames from which the ribs of the ship's cage are formed. These sections are then welded together to form the large modular building blocks used to build the ship. Once this is complete the whole block is moved to the Paint Shop where a second coat of paint is added, before the beginning of the miles of piping and electrical wiring that the ship is going to need is installed.

The *Ventura* would be made up of 74 prefabricated blocks, the largest of which would weigh 654 tonnes and be used to house some of the ships engineering spaces. In total there would be 21,000 tonnes of steel used in the *Ventura's* construction, which is approximately half of her displacement weight of 44,400 tonnes as a light ship. It is worth mentioning that that the ships gross tonnage does not bear any relation to the weight of steel in her construction. Gross tonnage is a measure of internal capacity which is measured by taking the total enclosed volume of the ship in cubic feet and dividing this number by 100; thus one gross tonne equals 100 cubic feet. Therefore the *Ventura* has a total capacity of 11,601,700 cubic feet or 116,017 gross tonnes.

THE KEEL IS LAID AND BLESSED

Around six months after the first steel was cut, the official keel laying ceremony took place on the 29th August 2006 which was attended by the P&O Cruises Chairman, Mr. David

The distinctive bow with its covered walkway is fitted to the **Ventura** *meaning that the construction of her forward hull is nearing completion. (Fincantieri)*

Dingle, and Fincantieri's Monfalcone Shipyard Manager, Mr. Carlo De Marco. The first block weighed 650 tonnes and was blessed by the shipyard priest, Father Gildo, before being lowered into the giant building dock where the ship was to be built. Once this had been laid the invited guests were treated to a lavish lunch provided by Fincantieri as construction continued on the new ship.

One of the first major stages of the construction of any new ship is the installation of the main engines and electric motors which will power the ship. They are some of the largest and most expensive parts of the construction project and need to be installed early on in the building of the new ship; otherwise the yard would have to leave large gaping holes in the steel work, delaying the construction of the new vessel. The *Ventura* is powered by a system known as diesel electric and this is the preferred choice of propulsion for most large new passenger ships. This is where very large diesel engines provide power to the ships electrical generators, which in turn provide energy for all of the ship's electrical needs. About 75% of the energy generated goes to the ship's propulsion and engineering requirements whilst the rest goes to the passenger, or hotel side of the ship. The engines on the *Ventura* were made by the Finnish company Wartsila who are renowned world leaders in marine propulsion systems and have engines in some of the words largest cruise ships and passenger ferries. Founded in 1834 in the small Finnish of , the company has its headquarters in and has grown into a leading global conglomerate in the energy business where it provides engines for one a third of all the world's shipping and has offices and factories in over 70 countries including and . Wartsilia produce a wide range of low and medium speed diesel engines for marine propulsion, and engine models are generally identified by the cylinder bore which is measured in centimeters and a V or L configuration to indicate whether the cylinders are formed into a V shape or are all in line. The slow speed engines are normally used in freight ships where one very large engine is used to power a single propeller, whilst passenger ships tend to go for multiple medium speed engines working on two or more propellers. The engines for the would be of two different sizes. Four of the engines would be 12V46C common rail engines each providing 12,600KW of power whilst two of the engines would be the smaller 8L46C providing 8,400KW of power. This would give the ship a total power output of 67,200 KW or just over 90,000 BHP.

ENGINES, PROPELLERS AND STABILIZERS

The technical team had also elected to use traditional shaft propellers and rudders and not the new and evolutionary Azipod pod propulsion system. Although Azipods offer smoother running and greater manoeuvrability, they are very expensive to build and maintain and were an unproven

*Left: A wonderful fish eye view of the **Ventura** and the building dock at Fincantieri's Monfalcone yard. (Mike O Dwyer)*

*The **Ventura**'s Bridge, minus her bridge wings is lifted into place. (Fincantieri)*

*The huge funnel assembly with its many exhaust pipes and assorted engineering machinery is lifted to the top of the **Ventura** in one of the last lifting processes of the ship's construction. (Mike O Dwyer)*

With the bridge almost in position it does not take too much imagination to picture the ship completed and ready for service. (Fincantieri)

All that's left to do is to give her a name so everyone will know what to call her. (Mike O Dwyer)

technology in 1996 when the design for the *Grand Princess* was being finalised. The *Ventura's* two propellers are LIPS 6 bladed FP propellers and are made of Cunial, a mixture of copper, nickel and aluminum. Each weighs nearly 40 tonnes and has 5.6 metre-wide blades which turn inwards towards one another which reduce the cavitational pulsing on the ship's hull and therefore give the passengers a smoother ride. Each propeller is powered by a Siemens 21 Megawatt electric motor which enables the *Ventura* to achieve a maximum speed of just over 22 knots. To assist with manoeuvrability, the *Ventura* has three 2,200KW bow thrusters and three 1,720KW stern thrusters which work in tandem with the two Wartsilia spade rudders which the Captain can control through a solitary leaver from the navigational bridge making all three systems work in one single operation.

For a ship as large as the *Ventura*, a tremendously sophisticated safety protection system is required as she will be able to carry over 4500 people at any one time and could be hundreds of miles from land when an incident occurs. The safety systems for the *Ventura* include such things as fire detection systems, sprinkler systems, fixed type carbon dioxide gas firefighting equipment, local water fog system, fire doors and water tight doors. In order to properly manage such a large volume of information at the time of an incident, Carnival Corporation had developed a Safety Management System (SMS) to systematically monitor and operate the safety and firefighting equipment used onboard.

According to the nature and the location of an accident, the system can present essential information in a clear and logical order to the Captain and crew with the procedures selected from a large number of predetermined options to assist them in implementing suitable procedures. For example, when a fire is detected, the system gives the location of the fire with the recommendations to control the relevant ventilation fans, fire dampers and fire doors. It is a highly sophisticated system and one which has been introduced on all of the Grand Class ships making them amongst the safest cruise ships in the world. The installation of this system begins with the construction of the engine room and forms part of the initial construction periods of the ship.

As cruise ships have increased in size, they have become more susceptible to the effects of strong winds and heavy seas as their passenger accommodation can create an air draft of around 50 metres. Despite this large superstructure, the centre of gravity of a modern cruise ship is relatively low, making them extremely stable vessels. This is due to the use of lightweight materials in the construction of the upper decks and the fact that the heaviest components of the ship, such as the engines, electric generators, propellers and fuel tanks, are below the waterline. When combined with the fact that these ships are proportionately wider than ships with deep drafts it becomes understandable why modern cruise ships are very comfortable in all but the most extreme of weather. To help improve stability and increase passenger comfort, the *Ventura* was fitted with a large set of retractable fin stabilizers that extend out from the ship's hull just a few feet under the surface of the water. Resembling small aeroplane wings, they are retracted when not required or when the ship is docking, and sit just in-front of the main engineering spaces. Made by Fincantieri's military division, they are computer controlled electro-hydraulic folding fins, weighing around 105 tonnes each and are tilted automatically as the ship begins to roll. The size of these fins eliminated the need for a second set of stabilizers which would have been more expensive and increased fuel consumption.

MILES OF WELD AND NO RIVITS

Once all of these major engineering projects were under way, work could begin on the job of constructing the modular blocks that would make up the main passenger decks; including the six decks exclusively for passenger cabins. Like the engineering spaces before them, each block would be built in the Fabrication Shop before being painted and lifted into position on the new ship by the yards two giant overhead cranes, which have a combined lifting capacity of over 700 tonnes. As each section was added to the superstructure, it was guided into position by a series of lasers which make sure that the block is in exactly the right place before it is welded to the ship. Welding steel segments together to form a large ship first began in the 1920's but it wasn't for another 30 years that it finally replaced the rivet as the primary method of ship construction. The hull of a large passenger ship built in the 1930's such as Cunard's the *Queen Elizabeth* and the *Queen Mary* were held together by millions of rivets. In comparison, the modular blocks of the *Ventura* would be held together by nearly 50 miles of weld and not a single rivet. Early concerns that welding would not be strong enough for an ocean-going ship soon dissipated as advanced welding techniques have made the weld seam stronger than the steel it is holding together. In fact, welded steel is so safe that had the *Titanic* been welded together instead of being of rivet construction, she would not have sunk when she hit the iceberg in 1912. The width of each seam depends on the size of the steel it is being attached to, but on average the width of a seam on the *Ventura* was between 4mm and 10 mm wide with the largest seams on the bottom of the ship's hull where most of the weight is supported.

A NEW SISTER BEFORE LAUNCH

Work on the Ventura progressed well throughout 2006 until the yard closed for its Christmas break on the 24th December. By then over 10,000 tonnes of steel had been used in her construction and work had reached up to the passenger cabins on Deck 8. As work recommenced in the New Year, a surprising announcement was made. On the 3rd of January, it was announced that P&O had signed a letter of intent with Fincantieri to build a sister ship to the *Ventura*, which was still over a year from completion. The new contract was worth around 480 Million Euros and stated that the new vessel would be delivered in the spring of 2010 and be a more traditional P&O ship when compared to the contemporary and family based *Ventura*. At the same time, further information about what passengers could expect on the new *Ventura* was released by the P&O Cruises Press Office. As well as a celebrity restaurant devised by Marco Pierre White, there would be an oriental restaurant called East which would offer Asian and Pacific cuisine as an alternative restaurant, as would Ramblas; a Spanish themed tapas and wine bar named after the famous boulevard in Barcelona offering traditional Spanish cuisine. On the entertainment side, the toy firm Scalextric were going to create a large version of the popular toy in the Havana Club at the rear of the ship, and a circus school holding workshops by performing teachers called Cirque Ventura would take place at the very top of the ship on deck 19. The ship would have a traditional British pub as well as a large theatre capable of staging West End-style productions and a whole deck of deluxe cabins, as well as a mixture of large suites and balconied cabins available for passengers to choose from.

Once the steelwork for the passenger cabins had been completed the shipyard turned their attention to the ships navigational bridge and the passenger areas made out of aluminium at the top of the ship. This included the large well-being area, the outside pool areas and the self-service restaurants which would occupy the rear of the passenger area. By April 2007 most of the steel work was completed and the task of giving the ship her outer coat of paint could now begin. Like all P&O Cruises' ships, the *Ventura* would be painted white with the traditional buff yellow funnel. The paint used is a special type, manufactured by Segma Coatings called Sigmadur 550 Gloss. It has a durable polyurethane finish which is designed to provide long-term colour and gloss retention of the superstructure and topside of the ship. Below the waterline a different kind of paint was used called Intersmooth 7465. Manufactured in the UK by International Marine Coatings, it is a self-polishing copolymer antifouling paint which provides protection from abrasion and corrosion, and minimises future maintenance costs. In total, there are over 300,000 litres of paint on the *Ventura* which will require a constant maintenance scheme, similar to the Fourth Railway Bridge, to keep it looking fresh and clean.

As the hull was being painted the final pieces of the ship passenger area were added around the funnel, including the vast children's area on deck 16, the White Room on deck 17, and the impressive Metropolis Bar high up on deck 18, giving unparalleled views out to sea over 50 metres above the waterline. Once the last pieces were added to the completed superstructure, it was possible to view the profile of the *Ventura* for the first time and appreciate just how large this magnificent new ship would be.

FLOATED UP IN THE TRADITIONAL FASHION

The ship was now ready to be floated up. This important milestone was reached on the 8th June 2007 when David Dingle, and the *Ventura's* chosen Madrina, Moira Lumsden, led the celebrations by welding a newly minted Two Pound silver coin and a new Euro to the foot of the ships main mast. This is a maritime tradition performed throughout the world which is supposed to bring good luck to a new vessel. Moira Lumsden was a travel agent for Thomas Cook Holidays, chosen by P&O Cruises to be the Madrina because she had sold the largest number of P&O Cruises holidays the previous year. Once the coins were in place the ship was blessed by Father Gildo before Ms Lumsden cut the cable holding a bottle of Italian Prosecco which then smashed against the hull. Amongst a cacophony of noise as the shipyard horns were sounded in celebration, the building docks giant sluice gates were opened to the sea and millions of litres of water were allowed to pour into the dry dock and start to fill the area where the *Ventura* was sitting. This is a far simpler and safer way of launching large ships than the more traditional method of pushing the hull into the water down an angled slope. After about five hours the amount of sea water in the dock equaled the weight of the *Ventura's* hull and as the equilibrium began to favour the sea water she gently lifted off of her construction blocks. Immediately the ship was afloat, engineers went inside the hull to check for leaks and any other defects which could compromise the vessel's safety. Once they confirmed that the hull was sound and there was enough

*The completed hull of the **Azura** sits in the building dock waiting for her floating up ceremony and her distinguished guests. (Fincantieri)*

With everything almost complete for the big day, the painters make sure that Azura's name stands proud on her hull. (Mike O Dwyer)

*On the 8th June 2007, a bottle of champagne was broken against the hull of the **Ventura** and the sluice gates to the building dock were opened to allow the sea to flood in. (Mike O Dwyer)*

*Once the **Ventura** was afloat her hull was towed round to the yards fitting out pier. (Mike O Dwyer)*

The Madrina for the Ventura was travel agent Moira Lumsden, who is seen with Carnival UK's Managing Director, David Dingle and the set of coins welded to the ships superstructure which is meant to bring it good luck. (Mike O Dwyer)

water in the building dock to safely move the ship without damaging her, several tugs were attached and the *Ventura* was carefully manoeuvred out of her building dock and round to the fitting out basin where she would be completed over the next nine months or so.

The outfitting of any new ship involves the installation of an enormous quantity of equipment, ranging from the navigational equipment on the bridge to the wash basins in the toilets. Before any of this equipment could be fitted to the *Ventura*, it was necessary to treat all the metal surfaces with various kinds of paint, enamels and resins which would provide a smooth and uniform surface to work on, as well as providing good sound and heat insulation and an excellent undercoat for the final covering. Once this has been completed work could begin on installing the luxurious interiors that had been designed and built to make the *Ventura* a well-appointed ship indeed. The delivery of all this equipment was meticulously planned, well in advance, so that each part arrived for installation in the shipyard just at the right time and in the right order. When considering the equipment in the ships galleys, theatre, well-being area, restaurants, bars and walkways then one can begin to imagine what a logistical predicament this can be.

PASSENGER CABINS

One of the principal jobs during the outfitting is the installation of the passenger cabins which are built by the Italian company Santarossa, who have a large purpose built factory close to the shipyard. The ship would have a total of 1546 passenger cabins and 650 crew cabins with each cabin being prefabricated off site then transported to the shipyard by road. All of the facilities expected to be found in a cabin such as the bathroom, lighting, carpets and the furniture are all assembled before the cabin leaves the factory. Each cabin has a pre-designated number and is built in a specific order ready to be installed on the ship at the appropriate time. As each cabin arrives at the shipyard it is taken straight to the ship then craned into position through a hole which has been

*The Madrina for the **Azura** was Amanda Dowds who is seen with Fincantieri's Chief Executive Officer, Giuseppe Bono at the float up ceremony. (Mike O Dwyer)*

specially left on each cabin deck, then manoeuvred into its designated position by hand. Shipyard workers then connect the cabins essential services such as the electricity and the water pipes to the cabin. Soft furnishings such as bedding and cushions are added later. The 880 passenger cabins with their own private balcony do not have the sliding doors fitted to the cabins as these form part of the ships superstructure and are added before the cabin arrives.

Once all of the cabins on a particular deck have been installed, the hole in the superstructure is welded shut and checks are then carried out by the shipyard and the owner to make sure that each cabin conforms to the necessary requirements and is to specification. Once each cabin is passed as completed it is sealed up so that it cannot be accidentally damaged during the rest of the construction period.

Whilst the cabins are being installed work continues on the testing of the major engineering components such as the engines, electrical generators and heating systems. Some of this work cannot take place until the ship goes on her first of two sets of sea trials towards the end of the year, but a lot of dry-bed testing can take place and proves invaluable once the sea trials start. Other equipment starts to arrive for example, the ovens and fridges for the restaurant galleys, the huge washing machines for the laundry rooms, the lighting and

*The **Azura's** Aqua Pool is seen before the protective decorative outer coating is applied (Brian D Smith)*

stage equipment for the theatre and so on. All of this is installed by the contractors working in harmony with the shipyard in order to make sure that the construction process is not slowed down by any unnecessary delays. The ship has to be finished on time or the owner could impose severe penalty clauses for late delivery of a ship which can run into thousands of pounds per day. On average around 40 tonnes of new equipment is added to the ship every day with the accumulative weight of all newly added equipment totaling over 11,000 tonnes.

FLOORS AND CEILINGS

A good guide to how a ship is progressing is by the installation of the ceilings and floors. One of the first and most intricate parts of the passenger areas to be installed are the ceilings, which in some rooms can cover the full width of the ship. They often have complicated geometric shapes and contain state of the art light, sound, safety and air conditioning systems. They have to be very robust and conform to the latest fire regulations yet be flexible so that they can absorb the movement of the ship in heavy seas. The same applies to a lot of the bulkhead fixings which too must be hardwearing and fire resistant, yet create a luxurious feel that the passengers will enjoy. In contrast, the installation of the flooring is the first indication that the ship is nearing completion as this will only start once the services, ceilings and walls have all been completed. A majority of the flooring of the *Ventura* is carpet manufactured by the British company Brintons of

Kidderminster. In total they supplied around 50,000 square metres of carpet, ranging from the biscuit coloured carpets in the cabin corridors with orange and grey swirls to the vibrant zebra pattern carpet in the Metropolis Bar. Brintons are true experts in designing and fitting carpets to passenger ships as they have supplied carpets and furnishings to over 250 ships and currently have a very full order book with various cruise companies across the world. In total there were almost twenty different types of floor finishes on the *Ventura* including Italian marble, decorative resins and fine woods, all supplied from reputable sustainable sources. The *Ventura* is both elegant and environmentally friendly. Most of the decorative resins are on the outside decks covering the wet areas, the recreation areas, and the area where lots of passengers will enjoy nothing more than the traditional British pastime of sunbathing. These resins not only meet all of the latest safety regulations but also protect the steel decks, as well as acting as an insulator against heat and noise. They can even be designed to look like the traditional teak deck which is far more expensive and not used very often on modern ships except on the outside staircases.

Another sign that a ship is nearing completion is when the fine artwork is installed around the vessel. The *Ventura* was to

Right: The upper most decks of modern cruise ships are made of aluminium to help reduce weight, lower the ships centre of gravity and increase stability. (Brian D Smith)

The cavernous cabin decks are marked out with each cabin ready for the completed modular until to be craned into position. (Brian D Smith)

*The **Azura** is seen at Fincantieri's fitting out quay around nine months before her completion. (Brian D Smith)*

Before the ship is delivered from her builders she is dry docked to allow her hull to be cleaned and inspected for any defects. (Brian D Smith)

have over 7000 paintings and installations commissioned by 55 different British artists, costing over £1 million. These would be displayed in the cabins and public areas, making her a floating exhibition of contemporary British artwork. For the first time on a P&O ship, the cabins would have canvasses decorating the walls instead of traditional prints and the three main staircases would each feature work by individual artists designed to provide passengers with perceptual experiences and visual illusions.

SEA TRIALS AND THE ADRIATIC

By December 2007 the outfitting of the *Ventura* was well underway with most of her fixtures and fittings now in place. The major works remaining were to commission the engineering side of the ship and for the painters, decorators, carpenters, electricians and other subcontractors to finish off their work and have it approved by both the shipyard and the owner. It was time for the *Ventura* to leave her place of birth and go out on her first set of sea trials, known as the Preliminary Sea Trials. Early on the morning of the 24th November, the *Ventura* left Monfalcone with around 800 people onboard, all with different tasks to perform and records to make. The ship still belonged to Fincantieri and was officially known as yard number 6132. She is manned by Fincantieri Officers including the yards own Captain, Claudio Bellich, and the yards Deputy Director, Giorgio Gomiero, who have overall responsibility for the sea trials. P&O Cruises officials were on board including the *Ventura*'s future Captain

and a number of her Senior Officers who in reverence to their Italian counterparts wore civilian clothing. The sea trials lasted for three days, and during that time various extreme manoeuvres were carried out, including putting the ship hard over at full speed and doing an emergency stop. She was run at 100% power over a measured mile so that her official top speed could be recorded and several emergencies, including a complete power failure, was simulated so that the ships safety features could be tested. To demonstrate the agility of the ship, the *Ventura* performed a "Williamson's Turn," to determine how well the ship would be able to turn around in the event of an onboard emergency. The "Zig Zag" test was also conducted to demonstrate the ship's ability to rapidly manoeuvre away from danger ahead, while still maintaining its forward course. Finally, noise and vibration tests were performed to ensure that there is proper insulation between all staterooms, corridors and public areas. Once the trails were completed the *Ventura* headed for Fincantieri's dry dock facility at the Italian port of Trieste where any adjustments to the ships stabilisers, propellers and thruster units could take place as well as the cleaning of the ship's hull.

After a short stay in Trieste, the *Ventura* was ready to go on her second set of sea trials on the 2nd December, which are also known as the Owners Acceptance Trials. This is where the *Ventura*'s crew takes control of her, and actually gets to drive the ship for the first time. Before they did this, an incline test was performed on the ship where her metacentric height was measured by moving a known weight across the ship and checking the movement of the hull at a predetermined height. This is how the ships centre of gravity is confirmed. Once this was completed the ship was taken out into the deep waters of the Adriatic Sea and the Ventura's new crew could play and have a lot of fun with their new toy. Of course there is a serious side to the trials and just as on the first set of trials lots of readings were logged by both P&O Cruises and the ship's classification society. The Ventura's two sea trials were a complete success as she did everything that she was supposed to do, performing very well in everything that was asked of her. Fincantieri had built a very good ship. Once everyone was satisfied that the ship had been fully tested and everything that could be logged had been written down, the ship was taken back to Monfalcone for the final phase of fitting out before her handover to P&O Cruises.

Once safely back at the shipyard the final remaining soft furnishings and fittings are added to the ship as the architects and the owner work with the yard to approve each section of the ship making sure that everything is to the highest standard before it is signed off as accepted. Only once everything has been confirmed as in good working order will the ship be formally accepted by her owner and arrangements made for the final payment to be made to the shipyard, as only once the ship is fully paid for will it be released by Fincantieri and officially become a P&O Cruises ship.

A FINCANTIERI TRADITION

Eventually the day came where the Ventura was to be handed over to her new owners and say goodbye to her place of birth. On the 28th March 2008, Micky Arison, the Chairman of Carnival Corporation, and other distinguished guests joined the ship for a night of celebration. Fincantieri provided a wonderful dinner as they celebrated handing over their 100th ship to its new owners. A restored building at the shipyard was transformed into a museum showing photographs and memorabilia of the previous 99 ships built by Fincantieri as well as the Ventura. P&O Cruses commissioned the photographer Mike O Dwyer to design a mosaic artwork of the Ventura as a gift to the yard which contained over 1300 pictures of the ship under construction, a copy of which was placed in the ship's atrium. The following day, at the stroke of Midday, the Italian and Fincantieri flags which had been flying proudly from the ships mast were lowered in a special ceremony and the P&O Cruises house flag and the Red Ensign were raised in their place. The final payment for the new ship was made by the parent company and the Ventura was now officially a P&O Cruises ship. Once everyone who was not travelling to Southampton had disembarked, the Ventura released her morning lines and in a grand traditional fanfare, which included Sara Brightman singing "Time To Say Goodbye" the Ventura slid gently away and departed her Italian Shipyard for the very last time. Her journey to Southampton took just over a week and on a very cold morning on the 6th April at about 06:00 the ship was off the Nab Tower at the entrance to the Solent. After the pilot

had been taken aboard, the ship waited until her pre-arranged arrival time of 10:00 before she slowly made her way up Southampton Water towards her home port. As she turned off the Isle of Wight and started the final part of her delivery voyage she was met by the two local tugs, the Adsteam Surrey and the Svitzer Sussex, whom began the traditional welcome for a new ship when they sprayed their two water cannons over the front and rear of the brand new ship.

DAME HELEN MIRREN NAMES THE VENTURA

Over the next ten days the Ventura was shown over to the travel trade and the British media as everyone was eager to get a first glimpse of the largest ship ever built for the British cruise market. During this time the Ventura undertook a number of short promotional cruises where members of the travel industry could get a firsthand experience of the ship it would be helping to promote. Finally the day arrived when the ship was to be officially named and on the evening of the 16th April 2008 the ship was christened by Dame Helen Mirren in a spectacular ceremony where she commanded a team of Royal Marine Commandoes who abseiled into the event before she said the magic words: "I name this ship the Ventura. May God bless her and all who sail in her." She then pressed a button and in front of 1500 especially invited guests including; the restaurateur Marco Pierre White, the actor Nicholas Lyndhurst and the Mayor of Southampton, a bottle of Tattinger Champagne was sent crashing against the ship's hull. The horn was sounded and confetti rained down before everyone enjoyed a gala dinner on board. The occasion was an extra-special one as all money raised during the event went to three different children's charities supported by Dame Helen and P&O Cruises: Barnardos, Kids Company and Naomi House.

TIME TO START AGAIN

On the 18th April, the Ventura departed Southampton on her maiden voyage which was a 14 night cruise to the Mediterranean. Even before the new ship had officially entered service, work had begun on her on her new sister ship which it had recently been announced was to be called the Azura. The steel cutting took place on the 13th May 2008 and her keel was laid down as yard number 6166 on the 27th October later that year. As a result of the operation of the Ventura a small number of modifications were made to the Azura. Firstly, her diesel engines were changed from common rail diesel engines to ordinary low pressure injected engines. Common rail diesel engines are more efficient and environmentally friendly however, they are more labour intensive and expensive to maintain. Also, the Azura would have a duck-tail fitted to her stern, the only one of the Grand Class of ships to have this feature. This is because although the Azura is not officially the largest of the Grand Class, this accolade goes to her sister, the Ventura, she is indeed the heaviest. Her increased weight is a result of the choice of

*On a glorious spring day in 2008, the **Ventura** is made ready for the first of her two sets of sea trials. (Mike O Dwyer)*

*As part of the advertising material released for the **Ventura**, a cutaway diagram showing the many features that the ship offered was created. (P&O Cruises)*

Two of the finest ships ever built to serve the British cruise market sit proudly together at their builders in early 2010. Cunard's **Queen Elizabeth** *and P&O Cruises'* **Azura** *represent an investment of nearly £1 Billion by the parent company Carnival Corporation. (Maurizio Eliseo, Trieste)*

*Top: Darcey Bussell led a troupe from the Royal Ballet during the naming ceremony for the **Azura** in April 2010. (Mike O Dwyer)*

Above: A pose with the Captain's hat is always popular at naming ceremonies. (Mike O Dwyer)

*Right: For the **Ventura**, the actress Helen Mirren was joined by a group of Royal Commandos to help name the ship. (Mile O Dwyer)*

fixtures, fittings and amenities chosen by P&O Cruises for the ship, and the addition of the duck-tail is simply to allow for additional modification to the ship in the future without the need to modify her hull. Her passenger areas would also be slightly different as the *Azura* was designed to appeal more to P&O's traditional client base and returning customers, whereas the *Ventura* was more of a family orientated ship designed to appeal to younger passengers and families. New features included the addition of a wine bar created by Olly Smith called the Glass House where passengers could sample over 100 wines from around the world. Atul Kochhar, a three

Michelin stars chef, was to be enlisted to create Sindhu, an Indian fine-dining restaurant on board, and the ship would also feature a dance floor in the centre of her main atrium where passengers would be able to dance throughout the day. There would be a New York-style show lounge at the rear of the ship and a modern interpretation on a London pub called Brodies, named after one of the founders of P&O back in 1837 towards the front. There would also be an outdoor spa terrace exclusively for adults called The Retreat where passengers could be pampered in a quiet and relaxing area at the very front of the ship. For the first time in the P&O

*The **Ventura** shows off her futuristic design as she heads towards the North Sea in the Netherlands. (Ruud Coster)*

*In her first season the **Ventura** visited the Croatian port of Dubrovnik where she is seen next to the Franjo Tuđman Bridge. (Neven Jerkovic)*

*An outstanding view of the **Azura** in the Mediterranean sun as she slows to drop her pilot off. (P&O Cruises)*

*The **Ventura** spends her last night at her builders before becoming a P&O Cruises ship the following morning. (Fincantieri)*

Cruises fleet, the *Azura* would feature eighteen single staterooms to cater for the growing number of people who wanted to go on a cruise by themselves, and an open air cinema screen situated on the top deck in front of the funnel would show blockbuster movies under the stars.

ROYAL BALLET DANCE FOR THE AZURA

As a result of improved efficiencies at Fincantieri and a desire to start work on the new *Queen Elizabeth* for Cunard Line as soon as possible, the hull of the *Azura* was finished in eight months compared to the eleven months required for the *Ventura*. Her floating up ceremony was performed on the 26th June 2009 by the ship's Madrina, Amanda Dowds, the wife of her future Captain, Keith Dowds. After, she was towed to the outfitting berth whilst the keel for the new Queen was laid in her place just ten days later. The *Azura* went on the first of her sea trials in December 2009 and, like her sister, was dry docked in Trieste before going on her Acceptance Trials a few days later. She was handed over to P&O Cruises on the 26th March and set sail for Southampton on the 31st March, arriving in her home port on the 7th April. She was christened three days later by her Godmother, Darcey Bussell, a former principal dancer of the Royal Ballet, who presented a dance performance by the Royal Ballet School before performing the traditional bottle breaking ceremony to christen the ship. The *Azura* set sail after being blessed by the Arch Deacon of Bournemouth on the 12th of April, on her

16 night maiden voyage to Venice and the Adriatic, a route she knew only too well as this is where she was built.

Since entering service, both the *Ventura* and *Azura* have spent the winter months in the Caribbean, undertaking a selection of fly cruises, with their summer seasons spent in Southampton cruising to the Mediterranean, the Norwegian Fjords and the Atlantic Coast. In 2014, the *Ventura* will be spending her summer months based in the Mediterranean offering a series of Fly Cruises from Venice and Savona whilst the *Azura* will continue to serve Southampton. Both ships have been well accepted by P&O Cruises' passengers and like all good cruise ships have a loyal band of passengers who regularly sail on them. They are wonderful ships which offer a contemporary cruise experience with stylish design and innovative and signature features which set them apart from other cruise ships. They have set the standard in providing high quality, affordable holidays for many people new to cruising who had never cruised with P&O Cruises before, whilst proving something new and exciting for their more traditional passengers. With the introduction of their two "Superliners", and the promise of an even larger ship in 2015, P&O Cruises have shown that they are determined to remain Britain's favourite cruise line for some time to come. Cruising from the UK has never been so enjoyable!

*Right: The majestic Norwegian Fjords provide the perfect backdrop as the **Ventura** sails in Geirangerfjord. (P&O Cruises)*

Azura & Ventura

Interior Design for the British Passenger

No matter what a ship looks like on the outside, it is her interiors that dictate whether or not she will be accepted by her passengers and deemed a success by her owners. In today's modern world of cruising, passengers have a lot more choice with a vast number of cruise lines and an abundance of cruise ships to choose from when deciding where to take their next holiday. Some will have particular favourites that they enjoy travelling on whilst others are more flexible in their decision making and will not be influenced by a cruise line and the branding of its ships. Whereas in the last century each cruise ship was an individual with vast differences between sister ships of the same company, most of today's new builds are identical in every detail apart from a change of colour scheme and choice of finishes. Of course this is all down to the cruise lines desire to offer a constant product of recognisably high standard across all of its fleet so that every passenger can know what to expect when they travel on one of its ships. To that end, modern ship designers can be constrained when it comes to designing the interiors, as any thoughts they might have on developing a new and individualist approach to a project must be balanced by the owners desire to use its branding throughout the ship, as well as the need to increasingly consider revenue potential.

As the cost of cruising continues to drop and the number of berths available to passengers continues to rise, cruise lines are continuingly looking at ways of raising extra revenue once people are on board their ships. When the *Oriana* entered service in 1995 there was no additional charge to use any of her facilities. On all cruise ships today, passengers have a varied choice of restaurants to eat in as well as large, impressive spa areas to indulge in, lawn clubs to enjoy, and private havana's where they can rest in peace and quiet. All these come at an additional price to the cost of a cruise and are deliberately designed into the ship to create additional revenue streams for the cruise line.

While designers have their own ideas and aspirations, they need to bear in mind not only the requirements of the ship owners but also the latest rules and regulations for cruise ships. Anti-slip materials are becoming more and more standard, as are non-combustible materials, even when not required by regulations. Durability is also key, as passengers have a tendency of scratching and damaging interiors without ever intending to do so, meaning that the list of materials available for designers to work with is getting smaller and smaller.

A MODERN SHIP FULL OF BRITISH TRADITION

Despite this, most of today's new cruise ships have a very impressive and luxurious feel to them which makes them destinations in their own right. The list of amenities available to passengers means that there is normally far more for them to do on board than in any destination that they might be sailing to. As a British company with almost all of its passengers coming from the UK, P&O Cruises are very mindful that any of its new ships must have a distinctly British feel, and must appeal to both its regular passengers as well as a new breed

*The atrium on the **Azura** is a combination of soft colours and luxurious finishes and was designed with some of P&O Cruises more traditional guests in mind. (Brian D Smith)*

Above: The library on both ships offers comfy wing backed chairs for passengers to relax and read in a peaceful location. (Mike O Dwyer)

Right: Indian marble arches to the world are the main feature of the ships atriums which are both contemporary and extravagant. (Mike O Dwyer)

of customers who are from an increasingly wide and diverse background. A hard task indeed, but that is why on any of their ships you will not find a swathe of strong, dominant colours or brash materials because these things are not appreciated by the British traveller. What you will find are quintessentially British touches such as the traditional pub, smaller dining areas, larger cabins with baths, and lots of quiet places to rest, all designed with soft, unobtrusive colours and subtle finishings to create the perfect environment that could be described as British elegance.

When P&O Cruises decided that they were going to build the Ventura and the Azura, they approached several of the world's leading marine architects and asked them to submit their ideas for the new ships. As the customer, P&O Cruises would explain what it was that they were looking for and what was the main function of the area that they were asking the designers to consider. For the *Ventura*, the brief for the architects was to make the ship contemporary and fun so that it would appeal to a younger passenger base, and in particular, to young families who would not necessarily have considered sailing with P&O Cruises. As is common with most new cruise ships of today, the number of places where people could choose to eat was to be increased with a specialty restaurant by a celebrity chef as the highlight of the gastronomic experience. There was to be a large well-being area at the forward end of the ship where passengers could not only

exercise on the most up-to-date training equipment but also an area of pure indulgence where passengers could enjoy sauna's, massages, aromatherapy and a whole host of things that would make them feel extra special. For the *Azura*, the design brief was similar, but for a more traditional P&O Cruises experience that would be more appealing to P&O Cruises' loyal and established customers.

AN ITALIAN ARCHITECT WITH A PROVEN PEDIGREE

As the Atrium is considered to be the heart of the ship and one of the most important areas, where passengers get their first impression of what life is like on board a P&O Cruises ship, it was decided to allow all the selected architects to submit individual ideas for this area. The theme was to be 'arches to the world' with four predominant arches set around a contemporary glass design with a reference to P&O Cruises' maritime history. Each architect would submit their design and P&O would then choose their preferred option. As the two new ships were to be a continuation of the Grand Class of ships, it was decided to use the renound Italian architect, Giacomo Mortola, as coordinating architect as he had been the lead architect on most of the Grand Class fleet and had a good working relationship with the shipyard Fincantieri and their suppliers. The project team then held several meetings with their chosen architect to decide which architects were to

*The **Ventura**'s Havana Room is the ship's show lounge which has a vibrant and authentically Cuban feel about it. (Brian D Smith)*

*Top: The **Azura**'s poolside bar has a Christmas feel to it as the ship's decorations give it a distinctly festive look. (Brian D Smith)*

*Above: Olli Smith's Glasshouse Bar on the **Azura** has repeatedly won the the Best Bar at Sea in an annual poll of British cruisers. (Brian D Smith)*

*Right: The Blue Bar on the **Azura** is a reflection of the Red Bar on the Ventura. (Brian D Smith)*

*The Planet Bar on the **Azura** is situated on Deck 18 and provides a fashionable place to relax with unrivalled views over the ships wake. (Brian D Smith)*

be chosen to design the new ships. In the end, four different design teams were chosen including Giacomo Mortloa's company of GEM SRL who were awarded the design for the restaurants, the theatre, the main bars and casino. The British company of SMC won the contract for the ship's cabins and children's areas, whilst another British company, Design Team, won the contract for the Atrium along with the associated reception areas, retail areas and bar and coffee shops. The last of the contracts went to the German firm, PartnerShip Design who were responsible for the open deck and pool areas, the well-being area, the show lounges and the photo gallery. All these companies had proven pedigrees in marine design and were considered to be the elite in their own specialist areas.

Unlike the *Oriana* and the *Aurora*, which had both been built as one-off ships, with their own unique interiors, the *Ventura* and the *Azura* would have to follow the same basic general arrangement as the previous units of the Grand Class, but with their own distinct finishes to give each ship a certain amount of individuality. In short, the two ships were going to be luxurious floating resorts that would appeal to everyone, although certain areas were to be designed to appeal more to some people than others.

A REAL BEAT AT THE HEART OF THE SHIP

When you enter the *Ventura* or the *Azura* it is usually by the main passenger gangway on Deck 5, which takes you straight to the atrium and the heart of the ship. It is here that you get your first appreciation of the immense size and dramatic architecture of these impressive new vessels. Rising through three decks with staircases sweeping down on each side, the atrium is framed by four black arched gateways, specially built from Indian granite in reverence to P&O Cruises' heritage. They are 9.3 metres high and are symbols of gateways to the world. Two panoramic glass lifts combine with pastel-coloured neon lights and a further abundance of glass to create a contemporary and welcoming atmosphere where passengers can emanate through to other public areas of the ship. Intricately designed marble floors harmonize with a splendid mixture of vibrantly coloured hand-woven rugs and works of art by Eoghan Bridge and Nick Munro to help create the sense of a modern-day luxury hotel. On the *Azura*, a wooden dance floor is situated at the base of the atrium where dance recitals can be conducted throughout the cruise, whilst on the *Ventura* a deep, rich red and beige carpet, with large shapes and swirls, combines with enormous arm-chairs

The Retreat is a well-being area where passengers can be pampered in opulent surroundings whilst enjoying a day in the Spa. (P&O Cruises)

and sofas to invite you to sit back and listen to the many musicians that play throughout the day. Dramatically illuminating, spotlights concealed in the ceiling help to focus this area's sense of drama and really create the spirit that makes you feel that the ship has a life and personality of its own.

An Italian styled coffee shop, Tazzine on *Ventura* and Java on *Azura*, is situated on the lowest level of each atrium where passengers can have morning coffee, afternoon tea or something stronger, and gives the atrium a sense of purpose as well as being the hub of the ship. A mixture of white and black marble floors complement the richly coloured brown and beige leather chairs that invite you to sit and enjoy the copious amounts of natural light that flood in from four large picture windows and the extraordinary views out to sea. On the other side of the atrium are the future cruise sales desks, the shore excursions desk, and the ships library that are all easily accessible and make sure that the atrium is always a hive of activity.

On the first floor of each atrium is the ship's reception desk and main retail outlets, whilst at the top of the atrium is the Blue Note Bar on *Azura* and the Red Note Bar on *Ventura*. Bright, colourful glass counters and rich marble and granite floors, real leather chairs and comfy sofas, mixed with crystal droplets around the ceiling, supports to create a popular place for passengers to enjoy a drink before or after dinner; no doubt due to its close proximity to two of the ships main restaurants.

PUBS, CLUBS AND OTHER ASSORTED BRITISH PASTIMES.

Moving away from the atriums on both ships you soon come across other particularly quaint, essential touches which make the *Ventura* and the *Azura* so distinctively British. Going forward on Deck 6 you come to one of the larger ships bars which has been designed to give the feel of a traditional British pub. With dark beams, tall bar stools, deep comfy furniture and other assortments that you would expect to find in an established country pub, they are a throwback to a P&O ritual that has been going on for years. On the *Ventura* the pub has a railway theme with the names of many famous British stations on display as well as a large model railway running around the top of the bar. On the *Azura*, it was decided to follow another old P&O tradition and name the bar after one of the company's founders, Brodie McGhie Willcox. This time simply named Brodies, high winged-back brightly coloured leather chairs blend with dark wooden bar stools grouped in fours around tall mahogany square tables, whilst black and white photos of London are displayed on the walls. The *Ventura* was given its fun factor with the inclusion of chandeliers in bright colours of red, blue, yellow, green and purple. Adjacent to the pub on both ships are the casinos which are considerably smaller than most large resort ships as gambling is not a major pastime for the British when they are on holiday, the size of the casinos simply reflects this.

At the very front of the ships are the 800 seat, traditional proscenium theatres known as the Playhouse on the *Azura* and the Arena on *Ventura*. Designed by Giacomo Mortola, these substantial rooms were intended to achieve an effective use of lighting and acoustics at the same time as providing the largest amount of unobscured sightlines for as many people as possible. Seating is of a low back design on one level which gently slopes up over two decks and is fitted out with plush deep red upholstery on the *Azura* but a more austere beige colour on the *Ventura*. On the staircases are large floor to ceiling mahogany panels that display the P&O Cruises emblem of the rising sun, and carpets of a particularly thick design so that the sounds of any late-comers to the show are not a distraction to other theatre goers. Unlike on other P&O Cruises ships, there are drinks holders in the seats which fold out to provide a handy table so that guests can enjoy a drink whilst watching the top quality entertainment the company provides for its passengers. The stage is over 25 metres wide and covers the full width of the theatre, whilst the fly loft used to move the scenery extends up as far as Deck 8.

FREEDOM, CLUB AND SELECT DINING ARE ALL PART OF THE GASTRONOMIC EXPERIENCE

One deck up, on the Promenade Deck, you come to the first of the ships select restaurants called Las Ramblas on the *Ventura* and The Glasshouse on the *Azura*. The Las Ramblas is a Spanish themed tapas bar, named after the famous boulevard in Barcelona and has a large traditional bar made of mahogany wood with a light brown marble top. Spanish wine

bottles are displayed around the top of the bar which is illuminated by discrete lighting from behind. Wooden beams in the ceiling combine with a bright red carpet, beige leather bar stools and lightly coloured formal furniture to create the feel of a Spanish villa, complete with its own patio area where you can even find a large tree to sit under and enjoy your meal.

On the *Azura* it was decided to go for something completely revolutionary in designing the Glasshouse in corroboration with the sommelier Olly Smith. While the standard of architectural design was remarkably high on both ships, it has to be said that the architecture in the Glasshouse was outstanding. It is a sophisticated, yet informal bar & restaurant with green neon lights hidden in large frosted glass ceiling partitions and a metallic bar which has a brown granite top covered in highly polished glass. The tables and chairs are oversized and a mixture of brightly coloured blood orange and dark yellows which work very well to create an eclectic yet very pleasant location. Large illuminated glass display cabinets present to you the 32 bottles of wine that were especially chosen by Olly Smith, including the Prosecco Colli Trevigiani Brut Sylvoz Le Colture NV, which is P&O Cruises' exclusive label. Thanks to the enomatic wine system on display behind the bar, passengers can select a glass of wine and know that it has been perfectly preserved and stored at the precise temperature to deliver the optimum glass every time. The concealed perimeter lighting successfully delivers a tranquil ambience which is perfect to enjoy one of the many great glasses of wine on offer, whether on its own or as an accompaniment to the select food menu specially created for

Hot stones in the thermal suite are a wonderful way to relax and unwind. (P&O Cruises)

*Top: Brodies Bar on Deck 6 of the **Azura** is named after one of P&O's founders, Brodie McGhie Willcox. (Mike O Dwyer)*

Above: The photographs displayed in Brodies are laid out on the floor prior to being installed. (Brian D Smith)

Right: Swash patterns are formed up on boards by the architects to give the owners a visual impression for their designs. (Mike O Dwyer)

the *Azura*. In recognition of the exceptionally high quality that went into the build of the Glasshouse, it was recently voted as the best bar on any cruise ship by the readers of the Cruise Critic website.

Only a few years ago, dining on a cruise ship did not require a lot of consideration as options were very limited in where you could go to eat. Everyone ate in the main restaurant whether it was breakfast, lunch or dinner. Today, almost all modern resort ships have an array of dining venues with a number of options that allow the passenger to have a

variety of dining experiences during the course of their cruise. Despite this, most passengers will still choose to eat in the ships main dining rooms and on the *Azura* and the *Ventura* these are divided into three restaurants, to which you will be allocated depending where your cabin is on the ship. The Saffron Restaurant, the Cinnamon Restaurant and the Bay Tree Restaurant on the *Ventura* simulate the Peninsular Restaurant, the Meridian Restaurant and the Oriental Restaurant on the *Azura*. The first two restaurants are exactly the same and

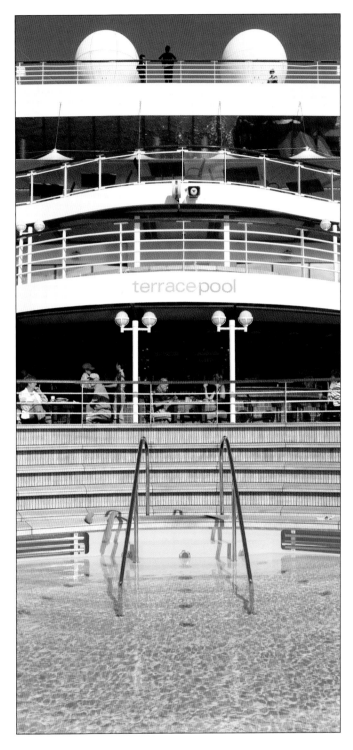

*Top: A delightful Spanish themed terrace is a feature of the Glasshouse Bar on the **Ventura**. (Mike O Dwyer)*

*Above: Dazzling glass display cases of some of the worlds most beautiful wines surround you in **Azura**'s Glasshouse Bar. (Brian D Smith)*

Right: The Terrace Pool is a wonderful sun trap where you relax and unwind whilst enjoying the ships outdoor facilities. (Brian D Smith)

situated on Decks 5 and 6 directly above one another next to the atrium. Walnut wood paneling features heavily in these restaurants with large colourful still-life paintings by the artist Paul Wright adorning the walls. Of these, only the Saffron and Peninsular Restaurants are open for breakfast, lunch and afternoon tea which are served on an open seating basis. Upon entering the restaurant the Maitre d' asks how many people are in your party and whether you would like to share a table before asking a waiter to guide you to a seat.

The breakfast menus contain a number of standard items that are available each morning as well as a daily special to vary the options a little. While the lunch menu changes daily, the afternoon tea maintains the tradition of familiar cakes, pastries, scones, and sandwiches. In the evening, all three main restaurants offer the same dinner menu. The cuisine and the style offered by P&O Cruises reflect the fact that a vast majority of their customers are from the UK, so although they offer a wide ranging menu with lots of different types and styles of food, it is predominantly of British origin and served

*The rich fabrics and colours of the Indian subcontinent provide the inspiration for the **Ventura**'s Tamarind Club on Deck 7. (P&O Cruises)*

*Top: The **Azura**'s show lounge is named Manhattan and is appropriately themed in bright, high energy American razzmatazz. (Mike O Dwyer)*

*Above: The **Azura**'s Medina Restaurant is the ships freedom dining venue where passengers can choose what time they would like to eat and with whom. (P&O Cruises)*

*Right: On several cruises each year you can find Marco Pierre White on board preparing meals for his White Room Restaurant on the **Azura**. (P&O Cruises)*

in the traditional P&O silver service way. For dinner each passenger is assigned to one of the three restaurants depending on where their cabin is situated on the ship. The Bay Tree, Saffron, Oriental and Meridian Restaurants follow the traditional passenger ship dining system, which P&O call Club Dining. The Cinnamon and Peninsular Restaurants follow a flexible dining system called Freedom Dining which allows people to come in any time between 6:00 and 9:30 and request the table size that they wish. If there are no tables available, they are given a pager and are beeped when there is a table available for them. Club Dining is where passengers sit at the same table every night with the same people at either a 18:30 seating, or the second 20:30 seating. Tables range from two to ten people, with small wall dividers carefully placed around the room to break up the restaurants, which stretch across the full width of the ship. The Bay Tree Restaurant and the Oriental Restaurant are situated at the rear of the main galley on Deck 6 and are only accessible via the rear staircase. They are the largest restaurants on the ship and are furnished with a more formal dark cherry wood, A light green carpet of patterned bay leaves is on the *Ventura* whilst an oriental pattern of red and green dots is used on the *Azura*. Each restaurant features two large murals by the Russian artist Valery Koroshilov, with other examples of his work especially commissioned for P&O Cruises also on display.

The ceramics and glassware in all of the restaurants was designed by the British designer, Nick Munro. Born in 1963 he studied engineering and design at the Imperial Collage of Science and Technology and the Royal College of Art in London. His career was launched when he transformed bedsprings into egg cups, which won him the UK Young Entrepreneur of the Year in 1987. He was contacted by P&O Cruises at an early stage of the *Ventura's* construction and asked to design all the things that go inside a ship from stem to stern, including the kettles and teapots in the cabins.

SANSKRIT LETTERING AND JAALI SCREENS HELP KEEP P&O CRUISES INDIAN HERITAGE ALIVE

The Promenade Deck on Deck 7 allows you to walk from the very front of the ship to the stern and includes a viewing area right over the bow. It is also the very top of the atrium, where a spacious wide gallery leads you to the first of the ship's show lounges. This open plan space has a bar, a stage, a dance floor and plenty of seats and tables to accommodate around 380 people. Decorated with a strong Indian theme, with brass cusped arches fashioned into Jaali screens to help divide the room into smaller, more intimate sections, most of the soft furnishings are a deep red, with green being used as a backing to the black chairs and tables. Large scatter cushions adorn the capacious sofas, reminiscent of many splendid Indian dwellings. Another interesting feature of this room is the use of Sanskrit lettering in the form of three triple brass rings on some of the support pillars along the length of the main gallery. Yet despite its superlatives of size and capacity, the

*The **Ventura**'s Oasis Pool is an adults only facility with a lap pool for the serious swimmer. (Mike O Dwyer)*

arrangement of numerous intimate seating groups with high back upholstered seating allow for some more intimate groups to enjoy the facilities whilst achieving some degree of privacy. Named the Tamarind Club on the *Ventura* after the Tamarind Tree which is found extensively is South Asia, the *Azura's* inference is named The Malabar, after one of India's northern states of Kerala. During the day, passengers can enjoy guest speakers or recitals in a quiet and relaxed atmosphere whilst at night the room takes on a more vigorous feel, with live performances enhanced by a state of the art light and sound system.

Next to the show lounge are the first of the ships truly select dining areas, and in keeping with the Indian theme of the Tamarind Club and The Malabar is the East Restaurant on the *Ventura* and Sindhu on the *Azura*. Both feature very heavy dark mahogany wood ceilings formed in a criss-cross pattern alongside the main isle way with a brass down lighter in the centre. Large square white marble columns are adjacent to highly polished metallic trestles with brown stone granite topes. The thoroughfare of the restaurant is a white and brown marble floor in a rectangular shape, whilst the seating area has a very plain deep rich red carpet. The tables are in square formation for four people, with matching chairs with cream leather upholstery. Along the sides of the restaurant are

Top: The entire deck on mini suites are a very popular feature on both ships with a wide range of comfortable features and a large balcony. *(P&O Cruises)*

Above: Polished wood and brass fittings set the mood for the occasion at the entrance to the **Ventura's** Oriental Restaurant. *(Brian D Smith)*

Right: The Lido Deck on the **Azura** includes bars, restaurants, swimming pools, Jacuzzis, plenty of sun bathing space and the first outside cinema screen for P&O Cruises *(Brian D Smith)*

Opposite page: The **Ventura's** atrium eludes an atmosphere of opulent and contemporary living that sets the character for the ship. *(Mike O Dwyer)*

*Top: The Glass House on the **Ventura** has a Spanish Terrace which was inspired by the ship's former Tapas Bar. (Brian D Smith)*

*Above: The **Ventura**'s East restaurant evokes your perception of the Orient with deep colours of reds and blacks with hanging globe lanterns. (Brian D Smith)*

*Right: Eoghan Bridge's sculpture "Joy" is part of a £1 Million art exhibition on permanent display throughout the **Ventura**. (Brian D Smith)*

The Arena Theatre proves comfortable seating on one level with uninterrupted sight lines throughout the auditorium. (Brian D Smith)

bench seating alcoves with dark brown bamboo separators suspended from the ceiling on two metal poles. Each alcove has a bare red wall which matches the carpet and a silver globe suspended above the table to give subtle lighting. The room has an oversized bar and windows at the rear which look out onto the Promenade Deck, allowing for excellent sea views to enhance the overall dining experience. There are two menus served here per cruise with the food on the *Azura* being overseen by Mitchelin Star Celebrity Chef Atul Kochhar, best known for running Benares Restaurant in Berkley Square.

As you move further back along the Promenade Deck you come to the Photo Gallery which is one of the largest establishments on any cruise ship. Staffed by ten professional photographers there are a number of large walnut display cabinets which have a wonderful display of 360 degree panoramic photographs taken by the British photographers Matt Wright and Chris George. Fifteen iconic locations from around the British Isles were chosen including; The Eden Project, HMS Victory and Edinburgh Castle. Perhaps the most remarkable photograph is that taken through the glass floor of the Spinnaker Tower in Portsmouth which has cleverly demonstrated the imposing height of this structure yet contrasted it with the traditional buildings of Old Portsmouth in the background. As well as the displays of traditionally printed photographs, there are a number of self-service machines where passengers can use an interactive computer screen to search for their own photographs before selecting the prints they wish to keep.

At the rear of the deck is the ship's main show lounge known as The Havana Bar on the *Ventura* and the Manhattan Bar on the *Azura*. Both are high-energy pluralistic rooms with a blend of artifacts and artwork relating to their respective cities. High-energy neon lights, which change colour with the mood of the day, are built into the bars, tables and room dividers. Dark woods mix with brickwork, polished metal and dazzling paint finishes, creating a very modern and alluring atmosphere in one of the largest rooms on the ship. The carpet is a yellow and black honeycombed pattern with beige leather seating around the back of the room and smaller, more intimate low backed heavy chairs arranged around individual tables as you get closer to the entertainment area. A substantial dance floor with state of the art lighting and sound systems and large flat screen televisions allows the room to be used for a multiple range of purposes including comedy shows, recitals and as the ship's night club late into the evening. For the *Ventura*, the photographer Paul Ward spent three weeks in Cuba photographing what he called an amazing, vibrant city with stunning architecture. His work is displayed in the form of very large black and white prints and smaller, highly detailed colour exposures that capture the passion and exuberance of Latin America. On *Azura* a large number of posters that originate from New York in the early part of the 20th Century adorn the oversized ceiling supports and walls.

LARGE CABINS AND LUXURY SUITES ARE THE PERFECT PLACE TO REST AFTER A DAY FULL OF ACTIVITY

The next six decks and the forward part of Deck 15 (there is no Deck 13 on either ship) are the cabin

The White Room high up on Deck 17 provides a terrace for passengers to enjoy the finest foods alfresco. (Brian D Smith)

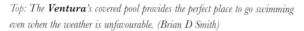

*Top: The **Ventura**'s covered pool provides the perfect place to go swimming even when the weather is unfavourable. (Brian D Smith)*

*Above: All the carpets on the **Ventura** were bright and colourful to make the ship a fun ship. (Brian D Smith)*

Right: A mixture of glass and teak wood make both ships safe and comfortable places for passengers to enjoy themselves. (Brian D Smith)

accommodation decks. Designed by SMC Design they are completely different from any previous P&O Cruises ship and contain a number of firsts for the company, such as original painted artwork in the cabins and the use of bright, bold colours instead of the more traditional cream and wood configuration that you used to find on a P&O ship. The carpets have interesting swirls on them and every cabin got what was, to all intents and purposes, a walk-in wardrobe with enough space for a large amount of clothing to be hung up with room to spare. Tea and coffee making facilities are also available in all grades of cabins and are one of the features that make the ships so British when compared to other lines. What is immediately apparent is that all of the cabins on these ships are significantly larger than most cruise ships, including the rest of the P&O Cruise fleet, with the basic inside cabin being 164 square feet compared to the industry standard of 150 square feet. The balconied cabins are a very generous 236 square feet including the veranda whilst the superior deluxe balcony cabins have over 310 square feet of space including a large bathroom and separate living area. In total, the *Ventura* has 1546 cabins with the *Azura* having an additional 18 single cabins bringing her total up to 1564, almost the same number as the *Oriana* and the *Aurora* combined. 88% of these are outside cabins with 880 cabins on the *Ventura* having their own balcony, compared to the *Azura* which has 890. The cabins on Deck 8 are a mixture of inside and outside cabins with *Azura's* additional ten balconied cabins situated at the very front of the ship. Some of the cabins are interlocking and have additional berths for up to four people. Deck 9 is an entire deck of superior deluxe cabins with balconies that extend two meters over the ships side and contain such amenities as a full size bath, two flat screen television sets and a separate living area with a large comfy sofa and coffee table. These cabins are extremely popular and with a welcoming bottle of Champagne and a box of chocolates waiting for you on arrival, they are designed to give you a sense of luxury that you would normally associate with a suite but at a more affordable price. Each have a robust colour-base of red and green with biscuit coloured carpets with high energy patterns woven into them.

For some a cabin is just a place to sleep and change, but for others it is a place to enjoy the ultimate in gracious living whilst relaxing at sea. The *Azura* and *Ventura* each have twenty four luxury suites, two family suites and two penthouse suites with over 750 square feet of space, more than three times the size of a standard balcony cabin. As well as the oversized double bed, there is a whirlpool bath, changing area, a large balcony with superior furniture, two flat screen televisions with DVD player and a dining table for four people where you can enjoy an exclusive menu served to you by your own private butler. Luxuriously finished in porcelain and polished granite, the bathrooms have twin basins, separate shower unit, heated towel rails and a range of personal toiletries from some of London's most renound establishments.

SWIMMING POOLS, WHIRLPOOLS AND SAUNAS ALL ADD UP TO A VERY ENJOYABLE EXPERIENCE

As cruise ships have increased in size, their owners have had to become very creative to accommodate the large number of people wishing to spend their time in the open air, especially on warm sea days, which can often put a lot of pressure on what is a premium commodity. The German company of PartnerShip Design were responsible for the Lido and Sun decks at the very top of the *Ventura* and *Azura*, offering a wide range of outdoor amenities. As neither ship has the tiered stern arrangement, which is so popular on some of the other P&O Cruises ships, the amount of space available to passengers wanting to sunbathe was always going to be a challenge. For other cruise lines this is not a problem, as most of their cliental are not British. But on P&O Cruises, over 95% of their passengers are British and one thing that the British like to do when they are on holiday is to spend time in the sun. As the *Ventura* was designed with families in mind, it was decided to build a large glass Megadrome over one of her two main swimming pools that would allow another favourite British pastime of swimming to take place even when the weather was not suitably favourable for such an activity. On the *Azura*, it was decided to replace the Megadrome with the first ever outdoor cinema screen on a British passenger ship. Similar to those on the other units of the Grand Class ship, the screen is a 300 square foot Panasonic Astrovision LED video screen, made up of small light emitting diodes which are visible even in broad daylight. Situated in front of the funnel just above the Aqua Pool, passengers can watch the latest films or popular sporting tournaments such as Premier League Football or Formula 1 Racing. The forward outdoor swimming pool has real teak wood for its surrounds and a hard wearing imitation teak simulant on the floor and is decorated in a predominantly sky-blue finish to reflect its natural environment. As well as an array of sun loungers, there are two fast food outlets and a bar offering a range of Pizzas, Hamburgers and Hot Dogs. In addition to the two main swimming pools there are four whirlpools and a third swimming pool at the rear of the Lido Deck which has space for sun loungers, built up like a small amphitheater on three levels. With real teak on the pool and the floor there is a waiter service bar and a seating area offering fantastic views over the ship's wake. There is also a sports court with deck markings for various outdoor pursuits including rings and a huge oversized chess set.

Also on the Lido Decks are the ships' immense self-service restaurants that span the full width of the ship for about a third of its length. In the centre are a set of serving islands which are mirrored on both sides of the ship in a formation that is designed to encourage people to move smoothly through the serving area and reduce delays. Each has a turquoise theme of light coloured furniture with tables for four by the windows and larger seating areas arranged in a circular shape with high back seating alongside the

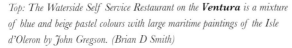

*Top: The Waterside Self Service Restaurant on the **Ventura** is a mixture of blue and beige pastel colours with large maritime paintings of the Isle d'Oleron by John Gregson. (Brian D Smith)*

*Above: The midships show lounge on both the **Azura** and **Ventura** has an oriental theme carried over to the windows and bulk heads. (Brian D Smith)*

*Right: A view from the top of the **Ventura**'s funnel taken on her return to Southampton after her first refit in 2013. (Brian D Smith)*

thoroughfare. Hydro maps of the world's oceans adorn the tabletops whilst large hand-painted murals inspired by the Isle d'Oleron by the artist John Gregson are on display on the *Ventura*, whereas on the *Azura* images from Venice are displayed in reverence to the name of the restaurant. Behind the main self-service restaurants are smaller dining venues, designed to offer additional capacity at busy times. Offering the same menu during the day, in the evening they become an informal alternative restaurant to passengers who do not wish to dine in the formal restaurants.

At the forward end of the Sun Deck are the ships well-being areas which are spread over two decks and offer a multitude of therapy and fitness options. With an abundance of natural light and an understated minimalistic approach, the entrance to the Oasis Spa is through an elegant reception area in a warm brown and biscuit scheme. To the left are the adult-only endless swimming pool and a private sunbathing area, as well as the sauna and steam rooms. To the right are the hairdressing salon and the entrance to the gymnasium, which has a glass wall to the ocean overlooking the bow as well as an extensive range of keep-fit equipment including treadmills, bicycles, free weights, and a very decent sized aerobics area. The treatment rooms are on the portside of the Spa whilst the Thermal suite is one deck down on the Lido Deck. Above the Spa on the Azura, it was decided to build the Retreat, an al-fresco spa terrace offering treatments under airy cabanas or simply a place to relax on plush loungers and your own steward to serve you with cold drinks and a selection of fine foods

The finest suites on the ships are open planned and designed to make your time at sea as comfortable as possible. (P&O Cruises).

THE ULTIMATE EXPERIENCE FOR CHILDREN AND ADULTS ALIKE

Behind the funnel on Deck 16 are the ship's vast children's areas which, when the *Ventura* entered service in 2008, were the first to offer the company's new children's Reef programme. At the entrance to the Reef are some brightly coloured figurines in a swimming pool and an illuminated fish motif that lights up the floor to the amusement of both adults and children alike. The Reef programme divides the under 18's into separate groups so that activities can be more easily managed and suited to their particular needs. Named Splashers for the 2 to 4 year olds, Surfers for the 5 to 8 year olds, Scubas for the 9 to 12 year olds and H2O for the teenagers, they each have their own dedicated room with an assortment of toys, games, Playstations and other activities aimed to make a stay on board the ships as enjoyable as possible. All the children's rooms were designed by SMC Design and feature soft, brightly coloured anti-slip materials and feature climbing frames and ball pools as well as an outside deck area where children can play under close supervision from the Reef Rangers.

Just above the children's area on Deck 17 are the ships premium alternative restaurants which have an identity all of their own. High above the sea, and well away from the activity of the lower decks, they provide exquisite fine-dining in the most opulent of surroundings. Named the White Room on the *Ventura* after the celebrity chef inspired menus of Marco Pierre White, the *Azura's* adaptation is named Seventeen after the deck number it is located on. Both are similarly decorated with dusky wood veneer and lit by a combination of low voltage and discrete pelmet lighting The tables are

permanently furnished with white cotton linin, Wedgewood bone china, Waterford crystal and sterling silverware. The room dividers are back lit with neon lights and are in an interesting wave formation and help create intimate alcoves where diners can enjoy a level of privacy not normally found on a ship of this size. The photographer Helen Sear was commissioned to photograph some of Britain's most famous buildings for the rooms whilst the Swiss sculpture Andreas Ruethi provided a resin and stainless steel monument called On the Tiles. At the rear of the restaurant is an outdoor al-fresco area, sheltered from sea breezes by a large orning similar to the structure found at Lords Cricket Ground, creating one of the most romantic places you could wish to dine. Both restaurants are the epitome of elegant fine dining and offer some of the finest cuisine at sea. They take P&O's dining experience to another level and offer passengers a chance to enjoy something extra-special that is guaranteed to be the highlight of their cruise.

Finally we arrive at the dizzy heights of Deck 18 and the Metropolis and Planet Bars at the aft of the ship which can bring passengers all the excitement of the world's most dramatic destinations via a 20 metre floor-to-ceiling video wall displaying cityscapes from around the world. At over 50 metres above sea level, the views from the large windows looking out to sea beyond the ships wake are simply breathtaking. A striking carpet and high-energy blue and red neon lights illuminate the bar in a dazzling array of colour which symbolize exactly what the *Ventura* and *Azura* proclaim to be: contemporary and luxurious on a scale never before seen on a British cruise ship. They are ships of their time and allowed P&O Cruises to increase the diverse demographic background of its passengers and make the company more appealing to the 21st century cruiser. They are indeed the Superliners designed for Britain.

*The **Azura** glides on a beautifully sunny Mediterranean Sea as she approaches the port of Ajaccio. (P&O Cruises)*

Azura & Ventura

Meet Your P&O Cruise Crew

Ship: The Azura. Position: Captain.
Name: Keith Dowds.
Age: 50 Years Old.
Country Of Origin: Northern Ireland.
Date Joined P&O Cruises: January 1990.
Date Joined the Azura: December 2009, as part of the new build team.
Previous P&O Ships: The *Arcadia, Aurora, Canberra, Oceana, Oriana, Victoria*, and *Ventura*.

Captain Keith Dowds knew at a very early age that he was going to have a career at sea as he was born on the banks of Belfast Lough in Northern Ireland, close to where some of the words most famous ships were built. He grew up in the beautiful coastal town of Carrickfergus in County Antrim before joining the oil giant BP in 1981, at the tender age of 17, as a Deck Cadet. He remained with the company for four years finishing up as a Third Officer before, in a surprise move, Captain Dowds decided to join the Northumbria Police Service in 1985 where he was based at their Whickham Station close to Newcastle Upon Tyne. He thoroughly enjoyed his work as a Police Officer but eventually he succumbed to the call of the sea and in 1989 he got a job with Ready Mixed Concrete working on their costal dredgers. After being promoted to Second Officer, Captain Dowds decided that he wanted another career change. This time he was to remain at sea but he was now going to work on large passenger ships. After seeing P&O's *Canberra* whilst on a family holiday to Sydney Australia he decided to contact the company to see if there were any job opportunities for him. An interview at their London Headquarters was quickly followed by a job offer as Third Officer on the *Canberra* which, by coincidence, he joined whilst she was in Sydney on her world cruise the following year. He remained on the *Canberra* before leaving to join the more intimate *Victoria* as Second Officer. In 1994 he left the *Victoria* to join P&O's new ship building team at the German shipyard of Meyer Werft where he was appointed First Officer on the nearly completed *Oriana*. After a successful period on the new ship he returned to Meyer Werft, this time as Safety Officer on the *Oriana's* larger sister, the *Aurora*. Captain Dowds remained on the *Aurora* working his way up to Staff Captain before being told on the day of the *Arcadia's* naming ceremony in 2005 that

Captain Keith Dowds. (Brian D Smith)

he was to be given his own command as Captain of the *Ocean Village* later that year. He would later return to P&O Cruises to command both the *Arcadia* and the *Ventura*.

In 2008 he was appointed Senior Master of his current ship, the *Azura*, which was still under construction at the Italian shipyard of Fincantieri, where in June 2009 he watched his wife Amanda perform the role of Madrina at the ships floating up ceremony. He successfully brought the *Azura* into service the following year and completed both her maiden seasons in Europe and the Caribbean.

When at home in Northern Ireland, Captain Dowds enjoys nothing more than spending time with his family and playing golf on one of Ulster's many fine golf courses.

DESCRIBE A TYPICAL DAY ONBOARD THE AZURA

It's difficult to outline a "typical" day on the *Azura* as it's quite true to say that no two days are ever the same. The main variation in my routines is brought about by the difference between a day at sea, or a port day. On a sea day I will usually be called by the Bridge at 07:00 to be given our overnight progress, the navigational situation, and the predicted weather conditions for the day. Once I have readied myself for the day I will spend the first hour in my office catching up on emails, checking my diary and preparing for the various meetings and events that are planned.

By around 09.00, I am in a position to make my daily rounds of the ship. This starts by visiting the Bridge to again check the navigational situation and progress towards our next port of call, along with confirming any times that may be relevant for our passage that day. Once I have satisfied myself that all is well, I then start a general walk round of the ship. The *Azura* is of course a very large vessel and this can easily occupy one or two hours of my morning, depending on which areas I visit. I like to try and include areas such as the buffet where passengers will be enjoying breakfast as this also allows me to chat and say hello and answer the many questions that people like to ask me.

It is equally important that I visit the many crew and operational areas around the ship, and I think passengers often forget just how much time this can occupy. The days of regularly seeing the Captain in passenger areas

Top: Low cloud drifts above the Ventura as she is captured on another visit to the Norwegian Fjords. (Ferry Publications Library)

Above: The Ventura pulls away from the quay as she departs the Croatian port of Dubrovnik. (Neven Jerkovic)

*Right: The bow of the **Ventura** edges out into Southampton water as Red Funnel's **Red Osprey** approaches her home port. (Andrew Cooke)*

are a thing of the past I'm afraid, the complexity of our operation is far removed from the days of old. During these tours of the ship I will always make a point of calling in to see the Chief Engineer, the Deputy Captain and the Executive Purser to catch up on any issues that require a face to face discussion, and to understand what may be going on within their Departments that day.

Once I have completed the walk round it is usually back to my Office to start the various meetings that invariably are scheduled to take place on days at sea, or to commence official ship inspections of the working areas, the food preparation areas etc. All areas of the ship are required to be

inspected on a weekly basis and this, combined with operational meetings, occupy a lot of time not only for me, but for the other Officers on board as well. My morning will now usually be over and I will take a break for lunch.

I am often asked by passengers just how much time I spend on the bridge. I think the expectation is that the Captain is there for large amounts of the day. The reality is, however, very different. I would say that less than 10% of my day, on a sea day, is spent on the Bridge. Obviously, this varies significantly dependent on the navigational area and the current sea and weather conditions. However, on an open sea passage in good weather and light traffic this would be typical. I have an extremely professional and competent team of Bridge Officers whom I can trust to navigate the ship whilst I am engaged in the numerous other duties that occupy my time.

After a lunch break, it's back into my office as its normally about this time that I carry out most of the administration-type tasks associated with the Captain's role. There will inevitably be emails from our Head Office to respond to and reports to complete, as well as the internal email traffic that arises from the large onboard organisation. Quite a lot of this will also relate to Personnel matters for which I have the assistance of another senior officer, our on board Human Resources Manager. As you can imagine, with a workforce of over 1200, the sorts of issues that come to light can be many and varied, and this is quite rightly an area of increased focus.

At around 5:30pm, I will make another brief visit to the bridge before getting ready for any evening functions and events, which are usually scheduled when possible for sea days. The various cocktail parties and passenger functions will mean I rarely complete my day before 21:00.

Before retiring, I will again visit the Bridge, and write my Night Orders. This is a traditional means of formally passing on my requirements for our overnight passage to the current and incoming Officers of the Watch.

A day in port will be most notably different due to my duties in maneuvering and berthing the ship. I will always be on the Bridge at least 30 minutes before we are scheduled to embark our local pilot and will then be actively involved in the navigation and handling of the ship. The local pilot rarely, if ever, actually maneuvers the ship. The complexity of our equipment and the characteristics of the ship are such that we depend on his local knowledge and advice, but the bridge team maintains control of the ship.

Once we have berthed, my day will often follow the course of a day at sea, with the obvious exception being that I will again be on the Bridge for our departure from port.

One of the aspects of my job that I love the most is that it is so varied, and therefore trying to outline a typical day is somewhat difficult, but this gives a good insight into a day on the *Azura* for the Captain. It is a very intense and demanding job, which gives me great deal of pleasure to perform.

Being in charge of a ship like the *Azura* is extremely satisfying and one which gives me a great deal of pride. If you see me walking around the ship please feel free to come up and say hello. It will always be my greatest pleasure to speak to you.

Ship: The Ventura. Position: Chief Engineer.
Name: Mike Jepson.
Age: 49 Years Old.
Country Of Origin: United Kingdom.
Date Joined P&O Cruises: September 1980.
Date Joined the Ventura: January 2010.
Previous P&O Ships: The original and current *Oriana, Canberra, Royal Princess, Star Princess, 2nd Arcadia, Victoria, Ocean Princess, Oceana* and *Ocean Village 1* and *2.*

Mike Jepson was born in the small Berkshire town of Wallingford, although he grew up in St Austell in Cornwall after his parents moved there when he was a small boy. After leaving Penrice Comprehensive School in 1980 he had a simple choice of following in his father's footsteps and working for the company English China Clays or following the boys next door's example and become an Engineer Cadet for a big shipping company. After choosing the latter he enrolled at the School of Maritime Studies in Plymouth as a P&O Group Cadet where he spent the next two years laying the foundations of what was to become a very rewarding career at sea. In June 1982, Mike got his first posting when he joined P&O bulk carrier, the *Jed Forest*, as an Engineering Cadet. After six months he was posted to the original *Oriana* where he got his first taste of working

Chief Engineer Mike Jepson. (Brian D Smith)

on large complex passenger ships. After completing his cadetship in Southampton the following year he was offered the job of Assistant Engineer Officer on the *Canberra*. This posting was to change his life in more ways than he could imagine as it was whilst serving on the *Oriana* that he met his future wife Lynne, who was working on board as a nurse. Over the years Mike has served on many P&O & Princess Cruises ships where he has successfully worked his way up the ranks to the role of Chief Engineer on the *Ocean Village 2* in 2007.

Mike and Lynne have been happily married now for over 20 years and have two wonderful daughters, Emily and Chloe. When not serving at sea, Mike likes nothing more than indulging in his passion for vintage motorcycles. He has built himself a large garage to house his unique collection of Kawasaki motorbikes, his pride amongst the collection being his Z900. He has recently toured from Land's End to John O Groats and attended the recent celebrations in Germany where they commemorated the 40th anniversary of arguably Kawasaki's most famous bike, the Z1.

DESCRIBE A TYPICAL DAY ON THE VENTURA

My day rarely starts at the same time, as I will be called by the Engine Control Room for "stand by" around 30 minutes before we arrive in port. The Chief Engineer, or Staff Chief Engineer, has to be present in the Engine Control Room whilst the ship is under "stand by" conditions, like the Captain has to be on the Bridge. It is very important at the start of each day to make sure I know what has happened during the night. Due to weather conditions we may have had to speed the ship up to avoid any unnecessary high seas, which can give the passengers an uncomfortable crossing, or to keep to our designated itinerary if we have been delayed for any reason. There could also be a technical issue with either the machinery or the hotel area of the ship which might require resolving quickly, early on in the day, especially if this will affect any of the passenger services.

Before 08:00 I try to quickly scan any emails that have been received during the night. Due to the ship operating in the Caribbean during the winter months there is a time difference of several hours from our Southampton Office which means that by the time I read it, the information can be quite old.

At 08:30 I hold a morning meeting with my officers to cover ongoing maintenance and any other issues that we have to discuss as a team. The rest of the day consists of duties that I am required to complete as the head of the technical department, such as attending the Senior Management Team meetings with the Captain, the Deputy Captain, the Executive Purser and the onboard Human Resources Manager. Also we have weekly inspections of the crew accommodation and onboard Public Health rounds of all areas of the ship. Whatever I am doing during the day, I always try and complete a full walk around of the machinery spaces so that I can see for myself how things are going and identify any maintenance issues early on. Whatever I am doing, I always ensure that I am available for the technical department if required.

There are numerous administrative duties that I am required to complete and some of the most important are the fuel logs depicting our daily fuel consumption. I have to monitor how much fuel we have on board and how much the next planned bunkering is going to require. The fuel is the most expensive aspect of our operation, and optimum performance is very important to make sure that we don't waste fuel unnecessarily. Today's marine engines are very fuel efficient compared to those being built only a few years ago and the *Ventura* has very efficient common rail diesel engines which, although they require more maintenance than a standard diesel engine, do offer far greater fuel performance.

When the ship is in port I have to attend the navigation bridge at least 30 minutes prior to departure where the Captain briefs me and his Bridge Team on the planned manoeuvre from that port, and we agree what engine configuration is best and the most economical for the passage. This is also a good time to discuss any other issues with the Captain, who I always see on a daily basis.

Once I am satisfied that the ship is ready to sail on a technical aspect I have to sign to confirm this. I then return to the Engine Control Room for the departure period and also brief my team on the manoeuvres we have agreed.

Most cruises are two weeks long and the ship will return to either Southampton or Barbados depending on the season. This is where we receive any technical spare parts that we do not have on board the ship. I have a very close liaison with our Technical Stores Manager in Southampton to monitor what is being ordered and received, and between us we monitor the various maintenance budgets to make sure that we are receiving what we need and are not paying too much for what we are accepting. Whilst in our home port we will also carry out our environmental discharges, such as the ships unrecyclable waste and used oil. As Chief Engineer I work closely with the Environmental Compliance Officer to make sure that we are complying with the very strict environmental regulations that apply to any discharge of waste products from the ship.

One of the more pleasurable aspects of my job are the opportunities I get to attend some of the important social events we hold here on the *Ventura*, such as the Captain's Welcome Onboard Party where the Captain and the other ship's officers have the chance to meet and chat with some of the passengers. I also get invited to the Peninsular Lunches, which are held for the passengers who regularly sail with us. During these social events, people like to ask me all sorts of questions about the ship and it is important that I am able to answer their questions, even if they are not within my sphere of operations. If there are regular passengers travelling who I know, I will often meet them before dinner in one of the lounges of the ship where we can enjoy some of the *Ventura's*

wonderful amenities on a more personal level.

I have worked for P&O Cruises for some time now and been at sea for most of my life. I have very much enjoyed my career and have worked with, and met, some wonderful people during that time. Being the Chief Engineer for a company like P&O Cruises and working on such a large and impressive ship such as the *Ventura* is privilege for which I am very grateful indeed.

Ship: The Ventura. Position: Executive Chef.
Name: Trevor Glass.
Age: 47 Years Old.
Country Of Origin: Northern Ireland.
Date Joined P&O Cruises: October 1989.
Date Joined the Ventura: April 2009.
Previous P&O Ships: The *Canberra, Sea Princess, Victoria, Oriana, Aurora,* the *3rd Arcadia, Oceana* and *Azura.*

Trevor Glass was born in the small Northern Ireland town of Gortin in County Tyrone. He went to Omagh High School before joining the Omagh Technical College in 1983 where his panache for cooking was noticed by none other than Clare Connery, who ran several of Northern Ireland's most popular delicatessens. After finishing college at 3:30pm Trevor would get in a taxi and travel the 75 miles to Belfast where he worked at Clare Connery's flagship establishment, gaining valuable experience which helped him to win a gold medal as part of Northern Ireland's Junior Chef Team at the Hotel Olympia Salon Culinaire in 1986, winning a gold medal.

Upon completing his education he decided to join the Army and served with the 5th Battalion Royal Enniskillen

*Top: Another view of the **Ventura** as she departs Dubrovnik and heads out into the Adriatic Sea. (Neven Jerkovic)*

*Above: Mike Jepson as an Engineer Cadet on board the SS **Oriana** in 1983. (Mike Jepson Collection)*

Dragoon Guards (Tank Regiment). However, Trevor quickly realised that he could better serve his country with his culinary skills rather than from the confines of a heavily armored military vehicle, so he returned to Omagh where he got his first job at the Royal Arms Hotel as a Second Chef. He later worked at the Silverbirch Hotel in Omagh and the Europa Hotel in Belfast. Trevor also worked for the BBC in Northern Ireland catering for some of their private functions. As Trevor gained experience in catering he wanted bigger challenges to advance his career so he moved to London where he worked at various large establishments such as the Tara Hotel Kensington and the Intercontinental Hotel in Portman Square.

Trevor was enjoying his work in the Capital but the allure of the sea was calling him. This he attributed to the fact that his Grandfather, Benjamin McKane, had been a fitter on the popular P&O ship, the *Canberra*. What Trevor needed was a job which would allow him to continue with his career in catering whilst satisfying his desire to go to sea. So, after much deliberation he decided to follow in his Grandfather's footsteps and applied for a job with P&O Cruises.

In 1989 Trevor was assigned as Second Cook on the same ship that his Grandfather had served on. He worked his way up to Second Chef before joining the *Sea Princess* in 1995 as a Sous Chef. He later worked on the *Victoria* before moving to the new *Oriana* where he was promoted to Premier Sous Chef. In 2000 he returned to the *Victoria* where he was again promoted, this time to Executive Chef. Trevor first served on the *Ventura* in April 2009 before joining the *Azura*, for her Maiden Season. After he successfully oversaw the many events and ceremonies which were held aboard P&O's new flagship he returned to the *Ventura* where he has firmly established himself as one of the premier chefs on the high seas.

When at home Trevor lives in Greysteel, County Londonderry, and has two sons, Trafford and Matthew Eric, who were named as a result of Trevor's love of Manchester United Football Club. He enjoys all sports and keeps himself very fit. When not working he likes to read or spend time in his garden and taking his family out to dinner, especially to Italian restaurants, which, apart from his own mothers cooking, is in his opinion, simply the best.

DESCRIBE A TYPICAL DAY ABOARD THE VENTURA:

Working for such a prestigious company as P&O Cruises is something which both my family and I are extremely proud of. The fact that I am lucky enough to be the Executive Chef on their largest and most impressive ship just makes my job

Executive Chef Trevor Glass. (Brian D Smith)

that little bit more special. Every day I wake around 06:45 and pour myself a cup of coffee whilst I check my e-mails and liaise with all the management both on-board the ship and ashore back in Southampton. Then I walk the ship's various galleys where I talk to my staff, especially the relevant Sous Chefs and the Night Chefs before they go off duty. Once we have discussed the previous evening's dinner services and how things went overnight in our 24 hour self-service restaurant, the Waterside, I return to my office to start some of the daily general administration work that I am responsible for. This will include a meeting with the various members of staff who are responsible for the different types of food we serve on the *Ventura*, including the Head Butcher, the Fish Cook, the Head Baker and the Executive Pastry Chef. We discuss the day's menus to make sure that we have enough stock onboard. It is here that I will authorize all of the appropriate ship's food stores requests which will include all of the meat, fish and vegetables that we will need to feed all of the passengers and the crew for the day.

By now it is normally around 09:30 and the morning's breakfast service is coming to an end. Once I am satisfied that no new problems have come to light, I take the opportunity to plan some of the future menus for the ship's three main restaurants and make sure that we have the necessary stores orders in place so that we do not run out of any produce during the cruise.

At 10:00 there is the daily galley management briefing where we discuss the day's business, making sure that everyone knows what we are going to be serving and what the requirements are for both the lunch and dinner service. It is also the opportunity for my heads of department to bring to my attention any problems that have arisen since the day started. At 10:15 I again walk all of the ships galleys and liaise with the Day Chefs, checking production, tasting dishes, and carrying out snap hygiene inspections to make sure everything is to my satisfaction.

At 11:00 I will check the ship's main restaurants prior to their opening for lunch at 11:30. Then we do what I call a menu presentation in the galleys where every dish we are serving is plated up so that I can check it for taste, quality and presentation. I do this in every galley before lunch and again before dinner. Once the restaurants are open for lunch I monitor them to make sure that everything is running smoothly and to offer any help and advice if it is needed. As I have such a good team working with me here on the *Ventura* I don't normally have to get involved, and any problems that arise are normally dealt with by the relevant head of department. The afternoon teas are looked after by the Duty Sous Chef which allows me to have my afternoon break from around 13:30. I use this time to relax and get something to eat or if I am in the mood use the ship's fantastic gymnasium. I will also use this time to get some sleep before the busy evening dinner service starts.

At 16:00 I am back on duty and checking my emails and actioning any outstanding stores issues that have arisen. I will again visit all of the ships galleys and talk to the team regarding that evening's dinner service and any other issues that have developed. Then it's time to check all the store rooms, making sure that we still have enough produce for the immediate future and that the correct stock rotation is being implemented. Once this is completed I return to the main restaurants for the two evening dinner services. Once the first dinner service is underway at 18:30 I will monitor all stations and liaise with all heads of departments to make sure that everything runs efficiently. During the service of the main course I will work the hot press carving the joints of meat or whatever else we are serving for our hungry passengers.

I will continue to monitor all aspects of the dinner service as the evening progresses which will include visits to all the ships galleys and a return to the hot press for the second dinner service.

By 21:30 the Night Chefs have started work and we discuss the day's events and what they can expect during the night. Once this has been completed and I am satisfied that the evening dinner service has passed off to everyone's complete satisfaction, I do one final round of all the ships food areas including all the prep rooms before signing off at around 22:00.

I will now give you some facts and figures which will give you some idea of the scale of operation that we run here on the *Ventura*.

As the Executive Chef, I am responsible for a team of 240 individuals who create more than 13,000 meals every day, for over 3000 passengers and 1200 crew. On an average 14 day cruise *Ventura's* passengers and crew will consume 40 tonnes of meat, 17 tonnes of fish, 80 tonnes of fresh fruit and vegetables, 3.5 tonnes of cheese, 4000 litres of ice cream, 16,500 yoghurts, 115,000 eggs, and 224,000 bread rolls. This will all be washed down with 2,850 bottles of wine, 10,000 pints of beer, and 14,000 cans of soft drinks.

I hope you have enjoyed reading about the work that we do here at P&O Cruises to make your cruise so special and such a memorable one. I look forward to meeting you and your family in one of the many restaurants we offer you here on the *Ventura*.

Above left: Even the Executive Chef cannot resist the temptation of freshly baked cakes. (Brian D Smith)

Above: Trevor Glass with some of his team in the preperation area on the **Ventura***. (Brian D Smith)*

Left: The White Room has some of the finest surroundings on any restautrant at sea. (Brian D Smith)

*The **Ventura** sits at the top of the Stockholm Archipelago right in the heart of the city.*
(Stockholm Chamber of Commerce)

Ship: The Ventura. Position: Senior Purser,
Passenger Services Manager.
Name: Jacqueline S Bott.
Age: 50 Years Old.
Country Of Origin: United Kingdom.
Date Joined P&O Cruises: April 1995.
Date Joined the Ventura: March 2007 (as part of the new build team in Monfalcone, Italy)
Previous P&O Ships: The *Canberra, Oriana, Victoria*, both *Arcadia 2* and *3, Ocean Village, Oceana, Adonia, Aurora* and *Artemis*.

Jacqueline S Bott hales from Staffordshire in the West Midlands but she was born in the county of Warwickshire in a small village called Newton Regis. After completing her education she moved to Tamworth, the home of both Sir Robert Peel and the famous Tamworth or Sandy Back Pig, where she went to work at the local branch of Barclay's Bank. She states that the superb training the bank gave its employees has stood her in good stead for all of her working life and been very beneficial for her career with P&O Cruises.

Although she was very happy working for Barclay's, a Mediterranean cruise on the *Canberra* in 1993 made her realise that there was more to life than a regular job with a big bank. So one dull and rainy Friday afternoon, when she was not having a good day at work, she made a phone call to one of the Officers she had remained in touch with from her cruise. This conversation was to change her life forever because during the course of it she casually asked if there were any jobs going at P&O Cruises. The response she received was extremely positive, being told that she would make an excellent Assistant Purser, so she decided that if she could keep her car and house then she would apply for a job at sea. After researching exactly what an Assistant Pursers role was she sent off her Curriculum Vitae to P&O Cruises in Southampton, but after a long wait received no reply. Undeterred, she made a phone call just before Christmas 1994 where she was told to resend her CV along with a covering letter.

At the beginning of 1995 Jackie again rang up to see if they had an update and was immediately offered an interview on a Monday afternoon in Southampton. She arrived at P&O's old offices at Richmond House where she was horrified to find out that did not have her name on the list of interviewees. Being a very determined girl she was not about to return to the Midlands without having an interview so she insisted that she be given an opportunity, after explaining that she had travelled a long way and spent the night in a hotel. The next minute, she was completing a typing test whilst looking out of the window over the dull grey sky and sea.

Her interview was very informal as she sat round a coffee table with a ship's Purser and a member of the human resources team. The interview went very well, but Jackie was advised that she would not be considered for the job unless she could type at least 100 words per minute and demonstrate good shorthand skills. She returned home and immediately enrolled in typing and shorthand lessons.

When her father picked her up from the airport after a short holiday in February 1995 he told her that he had been round to her house and there was a message on her answerphone from P&O Cruises advising her to call them as a matter of urgency. She raced home (mobile phones were still an expensive luxury in 1995) to see what the urgency was.

On phoning P&O, she was advised that a girl called Jane had walked down the gangway (resigned) on the *Canberra* whilst in Sydney and that they needed a Junior Assistant Purser when the ship returned to Southampton in April. Jackie was very excited and immediately handed her notice in at the bank. The rest, as they say, is history.

Jackie started her new job at the beginning of April 1995 when she boarded the *Canberra* in her home port and soon demonstrated that during her time with Barclay's she had developed not only a determined work ethic but also a wonderful touch when it came to dealing with the passengers.

In her 18 years with P&O Cruises Jackie has worked her way up to the rank of Senior Purser and served on many of their ships. She has a soft spot for the *Ventura* as she was part of the new build team completing her first Mediterranean and Caribbean Seasons back in 2008. She states that a big part about what makes working on a ship so exciting is both the people that you work with and the people that you meet, as well as the places you visit. In short, she is thoroughly

Jacqueline S Bott. (P&O Cruises)

enjoying her career and considers herself very fortunate to do a job which gives her so much pleasure.

DESCRIBE A TYPICAL 24 HOURS ABOARD THE VENTURA

How my day goes depends on whether it is a sea day or a day in port. If it is a sea day I will I usually start my day at about 07:30 when I scan through my emails to see if there is anything contentious in my in-box. I will then read the night log (details of the events from 22:00 onwards) to see if anything requires any follow-up that morning or if a passenger needs to be seen for whatever reason. During the night we have a Hotel Duty Officer who reports directly to me, so it is important that I touch base with them as soon as possible to see if there have been any issues raised during the night. I will then make my way around the department to see my line managers as well as the Executive Purser, the Commercial Manager and the Food & Beverage Manager. Once I have spoken to these people and confirmed there are no issues that require my immediate attention, I can settle down and start on my day's work.

I usually start by reading my stream of emails in order that I am prepared when I go and have my daily catch up with the Housekeeping Manager, Front of House Manager and Administration & Crew Logistics Manager. With the Housekeeping Manager I will discuss any operational issues, passenger situations or team welfare issues prior to visiting the Main Laundry to meet the Laundry Master and his team. The Front of House Manager is responsible for the ship's reception desk which of course is one of the most important areas on the ship, as it is the passengers' point of call for any queries or concerns they may have. The Administration & Crew Logistics Manager is responsible for the numerous amounts of paperwork which have to be completed on arrival in port and ensures all the formalities are followed for both passengers and crew disembarking the ship.

Once I have completed my daily catch up with the team I am happy, and return to my office to prioritise my work for the day, looking at what issues need immediate attention and need addressing with the relevant team members. There may be a need that I speak to a passenger about, regarding a complaint, whether it is a major problem with their cabin or a minor one about disembarking. On many occasions my team can deal with such complaints but some passengers are insistent on seeing the Passenger Services Manager as they believe they are the only person who can solve all their problems and will not talk to anyone else or disclose the reason for the conversation.

There will be various interdepartmental meetings that I have to attend, and usually the Executive Purser will hold a meeting after turnaround day to discuss the day itself and any items that we need to review in advance of them happening during the cruise, and to ensure that all is in order for operational matters. We usually have an Executive Committee Meeting, consisting of all senior officers across the shipboard structure, once per cruise, usually at the beginning, hosted by the Captain; once again discussing operational matters which need to be known to a wider audience. In addition, we have crew rounds, the inspection of crew cabins, spring clean rounds, the inspection of passenger cabins, and then we have the public health and hygiene rounds where we will inspect galleys, bars and pantries to ensure standards are being maintained.

My day will then continue to consist of meeting with the Commercial Manager, Food & Beverage Manager and Cruise Director, reviewing our up and coming one-day turnarounds in Barbados prior to meetings with the Executive Purser and other members of the team.

I may have personnel issues which need addressing sometime with the assistance from the Human Resources Manager on board. These can take only a few minutes or last quite a bit longer, you can never quite tell.

Normally I will finish work at about 19:00, however my office can be a hive of activity with people coming and going seeking guidance, advice and asking a copious amount of questions, which means that you can never guarantee what time you will finish. Prior to returning to my cabin I will see the Hotel Duty Officer to give them an update on the day and ensure all is in order in their world.

On port days I have to be in work about 30 minutes prior to arrival, to catch up with the Hotel Duty Officer and scan my emails to ensure nothing needs my immediate attention prior to heading to the gangway to meet our port agent. They are our representative in the port and our liaison if there are any problems that we need assistance from ashore to resolve, for instance a medical disembarkation. I also have to meet the Customs and Immigration Officials who will inspect the paperwork prepared by the Crew & Administration Manager prior to arrival. Once they have checked the paperwork and completed all of their formalities it is they who will give clearance for both the passengers and crew to go ashore. I then pass this on to the Bridge where an announcement is then made by the Captain or Deputy Captain advising passengers they are now able to go ashore, location of the gangways, details of the weather as well as a reminder of the time they are to be back on board.

If we have shuttle buses for a particular port of call, I am responsible for making sure that they run smoothly with the passengers disembarking in a safe and timely manner. Once this has all settled down I will then generally return to my office and commence my role for the day as detailed above. I will keep a close eye on the number of passengers that remain on board and monitor the peak times when passengers will be returning to ensure their journey is as smooth as possible. In tender ports this requires passengers to wait in the comfort of the public lounges before they are called and escorted to a tender boat which will take them ashore. This is usually a full morning process for a ship the size of the *Ventura* and involves many team members working together to make this as effortless a process as possible.

*The **Ventura** is clearly identifiable from her sister by the enclosed swimming pool area on the Lido Deck (Ferry Publications Library)*

Prior to departure from a port we have to ensure that all passengers and crew are back on board before departure and, on rare occasions, make the necessary arrangements to land the passports for those who will not be rejoining the ship for one reason or another. Our port agent will then liaise with them to make arrangements for them to rejoin the ship at our next port of call or return home at their own expense.

One of the things that I really enjoy about my job is the social aspect of it. We have Welcome on Board cocktail parties at the beginning of each cruise which is hosted by the Captain, where he introduces all of the ship's Executive Committee to the passengers. This gives you the opportunity to mix and socialise with passengers old and new on an informal basis. We also have the Peninsular Club luncheons for our regular passengers where I have the opportunity to sit and dine with them in a relaxed and social atmosphere. There is also the dedicated cocktail party which takes place on every cruise, which is always popular with the passengers and again a great opportunity to meet some of the people whom you have known over the years, or to meet new faces, some of whom have been cruising for years yet our paths have not yet crossed. This certainly allows for a great deal of reminiscing as to which people have come and gone and how ships and places have changed over the years.

On a sea day or a port day, once I have finished work and have no social functions to attend, I do like to meet up with passengers for a drink or a meal in one of the many restaurants we have here on the Ventura. Alternatively, if the mood takes me, I will meet up with a colleague in the crew areas and spend the evening just relaxing and having a private moment where I can let my hair down a bit. Either way, it is always very enjoyable and the perfect end to another great day.

I consider myself very fortunate to do the job that I do and have really enjoyed my time working with P&O Cruises. If you are ever onboard the *Ventura* and see me working around the ship please come and say hello, it will be my very pleasure to meet you.

Ship: The Ventura. Position: Youth Director.
Name: Lynne Bianchi.
Age: 37 Years Old.
Country Of Origin: United Kingdom.
Date Joined P&O Cruises: June 2005.
Date Joined the Ventura: March 2012.
Previous P&O Ships: The *Oriana, Oceana*, and the *Aurora*.

Lynn Bianchi was born in the seaside town of in the North East of England. She still lives in the area, in a town called Hebburn which is very close to Newcastle. She began childcare as soon as she left school by enrolling at her local college and completing her NNEB Nursery Nurse Diploma. Lynn managed to get a job at a local school, working with infant-age children which she loved very much. It was whilst she was working here that she was given the opportunity to work abroad for a year where she would be teaching English. To say that she enjoyed her time abroad would be an understatement. When Lynn returned to her teaching job in England, she realised she could not settle and had caught the travel bug. She knew there was a big wide world out there and wanted to go and see it. Despite this, Lynn knew her first love was working with children so she looked for a job where she could combine the two. Working for P&O Cruises on their biggest ship, specifically designed for families with young children could not be more perfect.

DESCRIBE A TYPICAL 24 HOURS ABOARD THE VENTURA

My day begins at 08:30 when I start work in the playroom as every day has a different theme and we decorate the room according to the theme. My personal favourite is Diner Day where we decorate the room as a Diner and the children work all day long to set the tables, make menus, and invitations etc. Then in the afternoon the Diner opens and the children all take on a job and serve their parents and special guests. It is a fantastic day and children of all ages gain so much from it. We also have theme days such as Pirate Day, Jungle Day, Teddy Bear Day, Chocolate Day and lots more. Once the room is decorated it is then time for me to check the morning emails and make the daily posters to advertise all of our day's events.

The playrooms are separated into age groups; Toy Box is for all children aged 2-4 years old and any children under 2 years of age and their parents. We then have Jumping Jacks for all children aged 5-8years. These rooms open at 09:00 and by 09.30 on a sea day we will have over half the children signed in with us giving the rooms the buzzing atmosphere that we love.

Once the playrooms are all set and ready to go, I then go around to our teen areas and help with set up. The teen's rooms are The Den for all 9-12year olds and Decibels for the 13-17 year olds and they both open at 1000. We don't run theme days with these older age groups because they do a lot more organised activities such as swimming, board games and quizzes. We then get all the day's activities ready to go before taking the 9-17year olds for breakfast. After I go back to the office where I get everything prepared for our afternoon events. This could involve planning a party and deciding what party games we will play and what music we should use or it could also be an event like our Family Mini Olympics so I then need to gather all of the equipment and type a running order. I'm then able to spend a little time in the playrooms with the younger children before going for an hour's lunch break.

After lunch I check any emails and send any communication between myself and the shore side management and other departments around the ship. The teenagers have their club swim at 14:00 so I head up to the pool area at this time to help out and make sure they are all set up and ready to go. The best thing about our job is that we can have fun with the children whilst we are caring for them! Once I'm sure that the club swim is running fine I will head back downstairs and set up the party or large event for the 2-8's. Pirate Party is my personal favourite because the children go around the ship on a huge hunt, find the pirates, and then we do the pirate duel, of course the stinky pirate always ends up in the pool.

After our main event it is usually time for Kids Tea which is held in the Waterside buffet restaurant. Here the parents can come and collect the children from us whilst they eat in a relaxed and child-friendly environment. We are very aware that the children can get bored really easily if they have to sit for a long time in the main restaurant, so this option is available for all who prefer a simple meal for the kids. If they choose this option then the children are free to come and join us in the playrooms for the evening activities whilst the adults eat in the main restaurants. The Youth staff and I pop up to Kids Tea as it gives us the opportunity to sit with many different families and chat to the parents as much as the kids. The playrooms remain open during this time for anyone's children who do not want to use Kids Tea, however this is a quiet time for us, so again I use some of this time to collect our cleaning equipment and stationary from our stores area before the children come running back for the evening session. It is at this point I will try to head off for a break and maybe go to the gym or go for some dinner.

It's then back for the evening shift, in which I try to spend time in the teens rooms as they hold their big games shows and pool parties. For the younger children we put on an evening movie which keeps them quietly occupied whilst their parents are enjoying their evening meal. If it's a busy summer holiday cruise and we have lots of children onboard we would hold a family disco or karaoke session for all ages, which is really busy and always lots of fun. I also try to catch up on a little bit of paperwork and future planning. My day normally comes to an end anywhere between 22:30 and midnight, and then it's time to catch up with my friends and colleagues before going to bed. It's a long day which can be quite hard work but I love it to bits and wouldn't change it for the world.

Lynne Bianchi. (Brian D Smith)

Ship: The Azura. Position: Fleet Environmental Compliance Officer.
Name: Robin Cooke.
Age: 48 Years Old.
Country Of Origin: Canada.
Date Joined P&O Cruises: January 2007.
Date Joined the Azura: February 2011.
Previous P&O Ships: The *Arcadia, Ocean Village 1* and *2, Oriana, Oceana, Queen Mary 2* and *Ventura.*

Robin Cooke is a proud Canadian National who has enjoyed a long and distinguished career at sea which has not only involved working on many passenger and cargo vessels over the years but also includes 25 years distinguished service with the Canadian Naval Reserves. He was born in the west coast city of Victoria, British Columbia, where he completed his formal education before studying Marine Engineering at the British Columbia Institute of Technology in Vancouver. Upon completing his education Robin got his first job with a company called Seaspan International Ltd which specialised in towing heavy objects from Canada to Mexico, a journey which could take up to 40 days to complete. After 13 years with the company, Robin moved to a subsidiary called Seaspan Cyprus as a Heavy Lift Barge Superintendent which specialised in the transportation of large marine objects such as oil rigs, large container cranes and mega luxury yachts. This involved Robin flying to all sorts of exciting destinations around the world, where he would supervise the dry docking and unloading of the company's ships, some of which had to be submerged to allow their valuable cargo to be floated off.

After 8 happy years with Seaspan Cyprus, Robin had attained his 3rd Class Motor Certificate, and although he was enjoying his job enormously it did not offer him the promotional opportunities that he desired. So after careful consideration he applied for a job with a small local company called Wayden Transportation who were based in Richmond, where he quickly gained his 2nd Class Motor Certificate.

By now Robin had over 15 years' experience in dealing with cargo and the transportation of large and valuable objects, but what he did lack was the experience with larger ships with a high horse power, which was a necessity if he was to achieve his 1st Class Motor Certificate. So in 2002 he applied for a job with British Columbia Ferries Services

Robin Cooke (Brian D Smith)

where he was responsible for the maintenance of their numerous car and passenger vessels which served the many islands and inlets of the Vancouver area. During his time with BC Ferries, Robin became the company lead for their new computerised maintenance planning system and was elected the President of their local trade union. He finally achieved his 1st Class Motor Certificate and became a Chief Engineer in January 2007.

Upon promotion to Chief Engineer, Robin wanted to work on larger and more complex passenger ships, so when a friend advised him of a position becoming available with Carnival UK during the summer of 2007 he had no hesitation in applying for the vacancy. After many phone calls, even more emails and several interviews, Robin started work for P&O Cruises on the *Arcadia* as Second Engineer. After a 4 month contract he was selected to join the *Ventura* as part of the new build team who would bring the company's new flagship into service. After a successful maiden season on the *Ventura,* Robin became the ships 2nd Ventilation Officer which involved looking after all the heating, refrigeration and air conditioning systems.

After being promoted to 1st Ventilation Officer, Robin was again promoted to Environmental Officer with one of P&O Cruises' sister companies called Ocean Village where he served on both the *Ocean Village 1* and the *Ocean Village 2.* When the *Ocean Village 2* transferred to P&O Cruises Australia in 2010 and became the *Pacific Dawn,* Robin re-joined the ship and achieved celebrity status when he came up with an ingenious solution to the problem of exhausted sea birds landing on his ship during their long and tiring migration. He recycled a wooden crate that had been used to deliver engine parts to the ship and turned it into a small Avery which he placed at a strategic part of the ship where the birds would not be disturbed. The Australian press loved the story, and pictures of Robin and his birdhouse were flashed across the world, giving much needed publicity to what is a serious problem for many migrating birds. After completing his contract down under Robin was repatriated to the UK where he joined the *Oriana* before serving back on the *Ventura* and finally joining his current ship, the *Azura,* now as one of P&O Cruises' Fleet Environmental

Compliance Officers in February 2011.

When not at sea, Robin lives in Thailand with his beautiful girlfriend who he met whilst serving on the *Ventura* back in 2008. He enjoys nothing more than exploring South East Asia, in particular Cambodia and Vietnam, which Robin describes as one of the most picturesque and tranquil parts of the world and, although he is delighted to call it home, he still has a soft spot for Canada and the delights of British Columbia.

DESCRIBE A TYPICAL DAY ON THE AZURA

My daily routine as a Fleet Environmental Compliance Officer is very similar to other ECO's across the fleet, and we like to say we are "Saving the planet, one day at a time." My morning starts in the office at 07:30 when I start the day by checking the overnight emails to make sure that nothing urgent or important is awaiting my immediate attention. This might include an email from another Environmental Officer in another time zone needing some help or advice with a problem, so this will get my attention first. Once that's completed it's off to the Garbage Room where I will chat to the staff I am responsible for to make sure that no important environmental or mechanical issues have arisen during the night. Then it's off to the Technical Office to see if the Chief Engineer or his staff has anything that they wish to discuss or bring to my attention. If necessary, I will attend the Technical Morning meeting if there are any issues relating to recycling or if someone wants my input on a particular matter, normally involving the Garbage Room. Then it's off to the Engine Control Room (ECR) to talk to the Watch Keepers and see how they are doing (as an Engineer, I kind of miss the engine room and enjoy talking "shop" with the Engineers). On my way out I'll grab the Oil Record Book and Garbage Record Book which detail the operation of the oily water separator and the transfers of bilge water/sludge and incinerator operations, as well as any food waste that was discharged during the previous 24 hours. These books will then get my expert scrutiny to ensure that all entries are written in the correct manner and are compliant with the company regulations. The readings are then confirmed to the Deck Officers on the bridge and the ECR. Whilst communicating with the bridge, I will ask the Navigator to confirm the ships position to ensure all discharges were made the legal distance from shore.

With all that completed, I'll go for a walk around Deck Four which is the main crew deck and always a hive of activity. Hopefully I will meet up with one of the Security Officers and see if they know of any issues I should be aware of (they seem to know everything). Then it's back to the office to see if any new meetings or appointments are pending. These could include the Operational Team Meeting where Senior Officers discuss any operational issues concerning the ship, as well as problems from the previous cruise and the passenger feedback that we have received. The Safety Officer and I will provide input and monitor any issues for any safety or possible environmental concerns. There is also the Health,

Environmental, Safety & Security meeting, the Public Health meeting, the Crew Welfare meeting or even the Navigational meeting. Once these meetings are complete, I will take the opportunity to carry out some basic environmental awareness training to new members of the crew who have not been on a cruise ship before or are in need in some refresher training.

After a short coffee break it's time to review all the other logs, reports and conduct inspections I have to complete and maintain as part of my daily duties.

This is the compliance aspect of the job where I record and log everything that leaves the ship, whether it is recycled, discharged into the sea or is incinerated. Then I conduct a full walk around the garbage room, which believe it or not, is huge and spans over four decks. I will check in with my Waste Disposal Supervisor, as they should now be progressing with some planned maintenance on the garbage room equipment that I have assigned to them, or be getting ready to land waste in our next port of call.

Once all this is complete I will usually find some time to do some future cruise planning. This does not mean I am deciding on my next vacation, but will be looking where I can next offload some of the ship's waste as all ports require 48 hours' notice before you can do this. I will also ask them if there have been any changes to their local environmental regulations as these can change without any prior notification from the port. If there have been any changes to the legislation then I need to brief all the relevant members of the crew who will be affected by these changes before we arrive. As you can see, the mornings in this job are very busy indeed as the one thing you can guarantee is that the garbage never stops arriving.

By now it is time for lunch and thankfully, most afternoons are a little slower. Now the garbage will have been off-loaded or the maintenance will be almost completed so it's time to close off and log all the paperwork for these important tasks. Then it's maybe a meeting with the Captain (my supervisor) or I'll meet up with the Safety Officer and we'll do a walk around and conduct some formal or informal rounds with the Department Heads. He will complete some of his safety rounds whilst I will be doing my environmental bit. Once this is complete I can relax a little and take the opportunity to walk around the ship and do what is known as a meet and greet with some of the crew and passengers. This is very enjoyable as it makes the whole job more sociable and it really is great fun talking to the passengers. Every few days or so, I will take the opportunity to pop down to the engine room and have a look around. If I'm lucky the First Engineer will not be too busy and I'll get to have a chin wag and talk shop with him for a bit.

The evenings are always busy for me but in a very different way to the mornings. I will start most evenings with a gym session as the wonderful food that P&O serve up for the crew can very quickly end up on my waistline. After dinner I can be seen at one of the many formal social events we have here on the *Azura*, like the popular cocktail parties. Here you will find me chatting to people about P&O Cruises' commitment to the environment and how we manage all the waste that a huge ship like the *Azura* can produce. The green strips on the rank epaulettes I wear do a good job of standing out and catching the eye of the passengers, which results in a lot of questions which I am always happy to answer. After, I might stop by the wardroom (I am President of the wardroom committee) and chat with some friends before calling it a night and retiring to my cabin. After a good night's sleep I get up and do it all over again, every day, 7 days a week right up to the end of my contract which can be anything up to 4 months. It is a demanding but rewarding job which I thoroughly enjoy. It is a very important job when you consider P&O Cruises commitment to the environment and all part of life on board a modern passenger ship. If you see me on my rounds or entertaining in any of our bars and restaurants then please come over and say hello, it will be a pleasure to meet you.

Ship: The Ventura. Position: Shore Excursions Manager.
Name: Tim Mathieson.
Age: 34 Years Old.
Country Of Origin: United Kingdom.
Date Joined P&O Cruises: January 2007.
Date Joined the Ventura: October 2008.
Previous P&O Ships: The *Aurora, Artemis, Oriana, Oceana, Ventura, Azura* and the current *Arcadia.*

Tim Mathieson grew up in the Hampshire town of Farnborough which is famous for the biannual air show which it shares with the French Capital. He went to the Salesian College founded in 1901 by the Salesians of Don Bosco where he achieved passes in 12 GCSE's in 1995 before moving on to Farnborough Sixth Form College to complete his A Levels. It was also about this time that Tim's skills as a footballer were being recognised as he joined Camberley Town Football Club as a left back, playing in the Allied Counties League. His future as a footballer was cut short when he decided to go to Leeds Metropolitan University where he attained a degree in Sports and Exercise Science. Upon completing his education he went to America where he participated in the "Camp America" project, spending six weeks in Wisconsin at a site looking after under privileged kids from Chicago. He was responsible for looking after a cabin of approximately ten 4 to 8 year olds where his duties included organising the various sports activities as well as acting as a lifeguard and part-time parent.

After a very rewarding time on the other side of the Atlantic, Tim returned to the UK where he got a job as an Operations Manager with the Prudential Ibis Club Leisure Complex in Reading where he assisted in the in the management of a multi-faceted sports, leisure and conference facility. It was whilst Tim was working for the Pru that a friend advised him of how good it was working on a cruise ship. He didn't hesitate, and immediately applied for a job with Princess

Cruises where he started his life at sea as a Junior Assistant Purser on a sister ship to the *Ventura*, the *Diamond Princess*. He went on to work on the *Grand Princess* and the *Coral Princess* where he finished up as an Assistant Purser before moving over to P&O Cruises as an Assistant Shore Excursions Manager on the *Aurora*, a ship he has a soft spot for as it was his first ship with P&O Cruises. Tim was promoted to his current role on the *Ventura* in 2010 meaning that he has now served on every ship in the fleet except the *Adonia*.

When not at sea, Tim loves nothing more than borrowing his mother's season ticket at St Mary's where he can watch his beloved Saints. He admits that life is going to be tough for them in the Premier League but he is convinced that they can make a go of it. Only time will tell.

DESCRIBE A TYPICAL DAY ON THE VENTURA

Like most of the crew on the *Ventura* my typical day depends on whether it is a sea day or a day in port. A typical sea day starts with getting into the office at around 08:30 in the morning to set the office up for the day. The first job of the day usually involves emptying the drop-box to process any booking forms that have been placed there overnight. Next, I will check my emails to see if there has been any correspondence from the Tour Operators for the ports that we are visiting during the cruise. For example, this correspondence might be regarding time changes, extra capacity, itinerary changes etc. I will also proof the ship's newspaper (the 'Horizon') for the following day and ensure that all of the tour related information is correct e.g. opening hours, tour advertisements etc. If the next day is a port day, I will also send all of the tour mustering arrangements to the Printer to include in the Ship's Newspaper.

Our desk opens at 09:00 and so, before we open, I will sit down with my 3 Assistant Managers and provide any relevant information, including specific tours that we have capacity on, and plan the day ahead.

At the beginning of the cruise, particularly on the first sea day, the desk is very busy throughout the day taking bookings from passengers and assisting with any queries or concerns regarding tours or the destinations that we are visiting. As the day progresses I will support the team where necessary and help man the desk over lunchtime when we start taking our lunch breaks.

If not on the desk serving passengers, I will spend the rest of my time in my office carrying out administrative duties and planning for the upcoming ports. A lot of my time is spent sending regular updates to the tour operators to keep them informed of how sales are going and requesting additional capacities for tours that are sold out, and deciding which tours to cancel. Also, as the cruise progresses I will prepare self-invoices to send to the tour operators and complete a variety of accounting and tour reports.

At the end of the day, once our tours desk has closed, I will assist the team in ensuring everything has been prepared for the following day. If we are in port the following day, we will prepare a dispatch sheet, which lists all of the tours in departure order and details the number of passengers on each tour. The dispatch sheet is our working document and is an essential part of the operations. Often we will issue stickers to passengers as they board the buses and so these need to be prepared the night before arriving into port. Before leaving the office, we will make sure that the booking form has been updated and all passenger correspondence and outstanding tickets are delivered to the accommodation office for distribution to passenger cabins.

Tim Mathieson (Brian D Smith)

Towards the end of the cruise, most of our time is spent completing end of cruise reports, dealing with any passenger issues or complaints regarding tours and planning ahead for the next cruise.

The Tours Team are very fortunate to be invited to attend many of the passenger cocktail parties that take place on various evenings throughout the cruise and this is something that we all look forward to very much. These usually take place on formal nights and include the Welcome On-board Cocktail Party hosted by the Captain. We are also very fortunate to be invited to attend the Peninsular Club lunches which are very lavish affairs especially for our most loyal passengers who are in the top two tiers of the Peninsular Club.

A port day is very busy for me and I am in the office by 07:00. Like everyone else my first duty of the day is to check my emails and then proceed to the gangway in time for our arrival. As soon as the ship has received clearance from the immigration officials, I will usually be one of the first people off the ship. Once ashore, I will meet with the tour operator/s and update them with our latest sales figures, and then either myself or a member of the tours team will inspect the tour transportation to ensure that it is in a satisfactory condition. As soon as the ship has been cleared, passengers will proceed ashore and we will direct them to their relevant tour bus or other form of transportation.

As part of the shore excursions team, another one of our duties is to escort the shore excursions guides and assist the passengers, as well as monitor the shore excursions programme and quality of the products that we offer. Therefore, the tour dispatch would be shared amongst the team and, working commitments permitting, we would each escort a tour whilst we are in port. When the tour that we are escorting is ready to depart, we would get on the bus or boat and introduce ourselves to the passengers as the ship's escort. Once we have done this, the tour is then conducted by the tour guide and we accompany the group as assist where necessary. This is definitely one of the perks of the jobs and it does put the passengers at ease to know that there is a ship's representative accompanying their tour in a foreign country.

At the end of the day, or once tour dispatch has finished, either myself or one of my team will sit down with the agent to count the tour tickets and complete a statement of carryings, which records the number of passengers on each tour. This document is then used by me to complete invoices that are forwarded back to Head Office in order to generate payment to the respective tour operators.

The tours desk will open again in the evening at approximately 16:30 and it will remain open for a couple of hours to give passengers the opportunity to book tours for the upcoming ports.

During these hours, we will sell tours, deal with any passenger enquiries and prepare for the following day if we are in port. One of our team will also go down to the quayside to welcome the last tours back to the ship. Once the last tour has returned we will radio the Bridge to confirm that all tours have safely returned. This is very important because we guarantee passengers that the ship will not leave port until all ship-organised excursions have returned to the ship, and I have never lost a passenger yet. Therefore, it is an essential part of my job when planning ahead for the cruise that I look at all of the tour timings and ensure that all tours are scheduled to return to the ship before the all on board time, in order not to delay the sailing time of the ship.

Once I have closed down the Tours desk for the evening I will relax with some of my friends on the ship and enjoy some of the facilities that we have here on the *Ventura*.

I really enjoy working for P&O Cruises and, as I have said, get to enjoy a lot of perks that make my job very rewarding. It is my pleasure to serve you when you are on the *Ventura* and I look forward to meeting you next time you wish to book a shore excursion.

The summer sun has not yet melted the snow on the mountains surrounding the Norwegian port of Flamm as the **Azura** makes a late spring call to a very popular destination. (Tomas Østberg-Jacobsen)

107

Azura & Ventura

Refining
Excellence

Over the last 30 years or so, the cruise ship has evolved from a basic small or mid-sized passenger vessel that held around 1000 passengers to the incredibly large and sophisticated resort ships that we see today. Whereas in the 1980's most cruise ships would only offer the predictable amenities that were fashionable at the time, today's ships are complex pieces of machinery that can hold over 6000 people and are deemed by many to be destinations in their own right. They are maintained by a group of highly skilled engineers whose job is to keep these ships in good working order and to deal with any problems that arise during the day-to-day running of these extraordinary vessels. Most of the maintenance can be carried out behind the scenes, away from the passengers, whilst the ship is in service, whether it is overhauling the main engines or one of the more mundane duties such as replacing one of the cooker heads in one of the ship's galleys. The ships are deliberately designed by the manufacturers so that much of the day-to-day maintenance can be carried out without taking the ship out of service, as the cost to the operator of having to do this can run into millions of pounds. Once, it was common practice for passenger ships to be dry docked annually, normally in the winter period, for around two weeks which was very costly to the cruise operator who not only had to pay for the refit but also had to lose two weeks' worth of passenger income. As time progressed and marine engineering advanced, it only became necessary to dry dock a ship once every two years and then every three years until we got to the current situation where most of the overhaul can be done without the need for a dry docking, and the ship is now only taken out of the water once every five years.

FIVE YEARS IN SERVICE REQUIRES A COMPULSORY DRY DOCKING

By the start of 2013 the *Ventura* was approaching her fifth birthday and the need to go for her first dry docking since entering service back in 2008. As plans for her overhaul were being put together it was decided to give her passenger areas a mini refurbishment as five years of intense service had identified what passengers had really liked about the new ship and what needed to be refined to make it more appealing to the travelling public. Both the *Ventura* and the *Azura* had been designed with different types of passengers in mind and both brought a number of innovative ideas that had not been tried on a British cruise ship before. Ideas such as the introduction of single cabins, a luxurious outside spa areas exclusively for adults, and even an outdoor cinema were all progressive yet not available on both ships. Therefore, whilst the *Ventura* was in dry dock, it was decided to introduce onto her some of the more popular features that had proved to be so successful on the *Azura*.

The British design team of SMC Design, lead by one of its managing partners, Andy Collier, were chosen to review both ships and to bring to life P&O Cruises realisations for the *Ventura*. From the autumn of 2012 onwards, a number of meetings took place on board the ship, and at P&O Cruises head offices in Southampton to decide what could be introduced onto the *Ventura* and how best it was to implement these ideas. As the number of people wishing to travel on their own was increasing, it was decided to add a total of eighteen new single berth cabins to the *Ventura*, bringing her in line not only with the *Azura*, but also a number of other P&O Cruises vessels that were now offering this

*The **Ventura** is seen in Dock 17 just a day after arriving at the Blhom and Voss shipyard in Germany. (Blhom and Voss)*

highly desirable feature. As the *Ventura* was the largest family-friendly ship serving the British market it was decided to introduce an adults only area where passengers could unwind, away from the excitement of such an eventful ship and be pampered in a more tranquil environment, high above the waves at the very forward end of the ship. A new dance floor was to be installed in the atrium and a new library built in place of the old cyber study, which would no longer be needed as Wi-Fi was to be introduced throughout the ship. A new perfumery was to be included, as was a new bar and restaurant called the Glasshouse which had been such a success on the *Azura* and recently voted as the most popular bar on any cruise ship. Other remedial work would include the replacement of some of the ships carpets and soft furnishings as well as new mattresses in all of the passenger cabins.

Of course the primary reason for any dry docking is to carry out the essential maintenance that cannot be undertaken whilst the ship is in service. This includes the major components of the propulsion system such as the thrusters, the propellers and the rudders as well as any of the external hull area that sits below the waterline. Historically, most of P&O Cruises' ships have gone to the Lloyd Werft facility in Germany for their dry dockings including most recently, the *Aurora* and the *Arcadia*. However, as the *Ventura* is such a wide ship at over 36 metres in breadth, she was too big for their dry dock, so it was decided to send her to Blhom and Voss in Hamburg, where the *Oriana* had been refurbished the previous year. Blohm and Voss have a proven track record in carrying out this type of conversion work and had recently carried out similar works to a great many cruise ships including the *Queen Mary 2* for Cunard Line and the *Balmoral* for Fred Olsen Line. Once the terms of the contract were agreed, preparation work began to make sure that everything was going to be in place so that when the ship arrived in Hamburg, work could begin immediately on her conversion as the time the ship was out of service had to be kept to the bare minimum. Orders were placed with the various suppliers who would be providing the new materials for the ship, including a great many suppliers from Britain who were involved in the original construction project such as Brintons of Kidderminster, who had supplied all of the carpets on the *Ventura*, as well as the numerous subcontractors who would carry out some of the more specialist work such as the installation of the new cabins.

Whilst the plans for the dry docking were being put into place, the *Ventura* was finishing off her winter season of Caribbean fly cruises from the port of Barbados. By the time she began her 4000 mile trip back across the Atlantic on 8th March, everything had been arranged for the ship to be taken out of service for a little over two weeks and for the sub-contractors, and engineers who would be working on the refurbishment to join the ship in Southampton ready for the journey to Hamburg. Once she had arrived back in the UK and her he passengers had disembarked, some of the material

that would be used during the refit such as the new carpets, light fittings and soft furnishings were loaded onto the ship in readiness for their installation in Germany. By the time the *Ventura* had departed Southampton at around 1500 on 22nd March, work had already begun to remove some of the fittings in the various areas that were to be refurbished.

THE PORT OF HAMBURG IS GERMANY'S GATEWAY TO THE WORLD, AND EUROPE'S THIRD LARGEST PORT

Sailing at just under 20 knots, the *Ventura* headed out into the English Channel and across to the French coast as all eastbound traffic has to travel on the south side of the English Channel since the introduction of the Traffic Separation Scheme in the early 1970's. Passing through the Dover Straights at around midnight, the *Ventura* headed up into the North Sea and along the Dutch coast before arriving opposite the German town of Brunsbuttel early in the evening. Here she was required to reduce speed for the 45 mile journey down the River Elbe, to the centre of Hamburg and Europe's third largest port (after Rotterdam and Antwerp) which is home to a number of Germany's most famous shipyards.

On arrival, the ship was met by a combination of strong winds and powerful tides which meant that she could not progress straight into her dry dock as planned but had to moor up on the north side of the river opposite the Blhom and Voss shipyard until it was safe for her to do so. Here her lifeboats were unloaded and sailed under their own power into the yard where they would be overhauled and given a new gel coating which would protect them from the harsh elements of the open sea for another five years. Once the winds and tide had abated the following day, the yard's pilot boarded the ship and carefully manoeuvred her into dock number 17, which is the largest dry dock at the facility and capable of holding ships of up to 350 metres in length and over 300,000 tonnes deadweight.

Once the *Ventura* was in position above her support blocks the ballast water in the dock was pumped out and her hull was gently lowered until it made contact with the top of the support blocks, leaving the *Ventura* about one metre above the dock floor. Once the ship was safely on her blocks, various lines were put ashore including telephone and electrical supplies and an air bridge was placed across to Deck 5 so that workers could get safe access to the passenger accommodation.

One of the first jobs to do once the ship was docked was

*Page 110: Work on the **Ventura**'s three bow thruster units can only take place when the ship is dry docked. (Brian D Smith)*

*Page 111: The **Ventura**'s bulbus bow and lower hull has just been repainted as work begins on her anchor chains. (Brian D Smith)*

*Opposite page: At night the newly painted hull of the **Ventura** glistens in the shipyard lights. (Brian D Smith)*

*With her paint work complete, the **Ventura** waits for her dock to be partially flooded to allow for her life boats to be returned to their davits. (Brian D Smith)*

the removal of two of the five bow and stern thrusters which are situated around 1 metre above the keel line of the ship. As these units are extremely vulnerable to any debris that might come into contact with the ship, they are recessed slightly into the hull and protected by a series of heavy duty steel bars which are welded across the width of the thrusters blades. These have to be cut away to allow the unit to be removed and transferred to the workshops where they will have their bearings replaced, their blades polished and be fully serviced. The remaining thrusters units were serviced in situ as they were not in such an advanced state of wear and tear as the two other units. Another important job is the maintenance on the ship's two folding fin stabilizers. The large amount of hydraulic fluid that is needed to operate them is drained out and the fins supported on jacks from the dock floor. The motors, hydraulic rams and other moving parts were all inspected and serviced and the seals replaced before being put back together again. Whilst this was going on, the shipside valves were looked at and serviced and a number of minor repairs made to the ship's hull.

In the passenger areas on Deck 5, the carpets in the atrium were removed and in their place, a new wooden dance floor laid. Made out of a mixture of walnut, ash, maple and oak, the floor was designed to be both durable and beautiful, as it had to host dance lessons and recitals every day for the next five years. Despite its continued heavy usage, it had to remain immaculate, as it was now the signature feature of the atrium and would help create the spirit of the ship that passengers would remember and enjoy long after their cruise had finished.

On Deck 6 in the Exchange bar, a whole wall of brick arches was removed so that the foundations for the eighteen new single cabins could be laid. The cabins were to be built in a similar fashion to the rest of the cabins on the *Ventura* and not the more modular design that had been tried on the *Azura*. There would be twelve outside cabins and six slightly larger inside cabins that would have plenty of space, their own tea making facilities, a flat screen television and a larger than normal bed, making them very comfortable and as a result, one of the first cabin grades to sell out on every cruise. Once the cabins had been installed, the brick arches were to be re-introduced, and so returning the Exchange Bar to its former glory.

On Deck 7, the dark wooden beams in the Las Ramblas bar were painted out and some of the soft furnishings removed. In the bar area, preparations were made for a new enomatic wine system to be introduced that would display 12 bottles of wine, chosen by the celebrity sommelier, Olly Smith. These would be kept in perfect conditions and at the perfect temperature ready for passengers to enjoy by the glass at any time. As well as a makeover for the bar area, new plush black

wicker furniture was introduced on the patio, with richly coloured scatter cushions providing additional comfort for those that wanted to dine alfresco without actually going outside. Renamed the Glasshouse, this new bar and restaurant would be complimented by a new and exciting food menu which would be chosen by Olly Smith to compliment his choice of wines. As work on the Glasshouse progressed, a selection of these new menus were tried out on some of the contractors, as Mr Smith himself joined the ship for the final stages of the refit and even sailed back to Southampton on her, ready to launch his new bar to the waiting media back in the UK.

Up on the outside passenger decks, the teak floors were sanded down and given a new coat of varnish. The swimming pools were drained and given a new finish that was hard wearing and easy to maintain, and the new enomatic wine system that had been introduced in the Glasshouse was added to the Waterside Restaurant. Throughout the ship, some of the more heavily worn carpets were replaced, including the stairwells, the cabin corridors and the lift lobbies.

At the very front of Deck 17, overlooking the ships navigational bridge, a sumptuous open-air spa terrace with sun loungers, a separate swimming pool and stunning sea views for use exclusively by adults was installed. With unobtrusive sun screens, a grass-like floor, an eclectic mix of oversized plant pots and a lot of space for those wishing to enjoy this well-appointed facility, the Retreat offered a new outdoor facility that was more inclined to a luxury yacht than a large resort ship and offered something completely new for the passengers that were looking for something extra-special to enhance their cruise experience.

Back in the dry dock, the ships fixed bladed propellers and her stern propeller shafts, known as tail shafts, were removed. This was to allow the blades of each propeller to be dismantled, cleaned and polished, and for the stem seals around the propeller shafts, which stop sea water flooding into the ship, to be replaced and upgraded. Work would also take place on the *Ventura's* two rudders, although this would be done it situ as it was not necessary to remove the actual rudders to carry out the required works on them. Once this was completed, the *Ventura's* hull was given a full renovation as five years of algae and other sea growth, which affects a ships performance considerably, had attached itself to the metalwork and had to be blasted off with high power water hoses. Once the hull had been cleaned, a special kind of paint, designed by the Japanese company Nippon Paints to be self-polishing, was applied over the hull including the bulbous bow, rudders and stabilizers. This not only protects the ship from the corrosive power of the sea but also forms a protective barrier against future sea growth and makes the ship more slippery through the water, which improves fuel economy. In total around 6000 litres of paint were used to repaint the *Ventura* to make sure she looked as new and glamorous as the day she entered service.

*Opposite page: The **Ventura**'s propellers gleam as all of the ships underwater propulsion systems are overhauled, repainted and prepared for another five years of service. (Brian D Smith)*

AS GOOD AS NEW AND READY FOR ANOTHER FIVE YEARS

By the start of the second week of the dry docking, everything was going to plan, even if it was a little behind schedule due to the 24 hours lost to the late dry docking. Eventually all the work that needed to be carried out on the ship's hull was completed and the *Ventura* was prepared for the dock to be flooded and for her to return to the sea. The tail shafts were reattached to the main propeller shafts and the propellers reassembled and attached to the ship. All the new engineering equipment was tested and commissioned and the thruster units re-installed and their protective grates welded back into place. The newly built passenger cabins and Glasshouse Bar were completed and accepted by P&O Cruises before the last of the carpets were laid and the new furniture for the atrium and spa area installed.

Once the checks to make sure that the ship's hull was sound were completed, the giant dock that the *Ventura* had been sitting in was partially flooded to a depth of five metres, to allow for some additional testing of the propulsion system to be carried out, and for the lifeboats to be placed back in their davits. By 17.00 on 4th April, all the lifeboats were back on board and the dock was fully flooded, allowing the Ventura to float again just before 20.00. As midnight approached, the dock head was removed and two tugs attached to the stern of the ship. The pilot was back on the bridge and slowly but surely, the Ventura was backed out of her berth and into the River Elbe before starting her 600 mile journey back to Southampton.

Once clear of the Elbe's estuary the *Ventura's* speed was increased to 20 knots, allowing her to arrive off the Nab Tower at the entrance to the Solent just after 0400 on 6th April. She proceeded up Southampton Water and docked at the new Ocean Terminal around two hours later where she was not scheduled to depart on her next cruise until the following evening. This gave P&O Cruises the opportunity to show off their ship to invited guests and members of the cruise and travel trade who were all eager to see how the new-look *Ventura* had been improved and what passengers could expect to see when they sailed on her. Everyone thought the ship looked fantastic and that the refit had gone a long way to making sure that the *Ventura* remained a very desirable ship for passengers to enjoy cruising on for the foreseeable future.

The *Ventura* is now in her sixth year in service and is a very popular ship with both her passengers and crew. She has a loyal band of followers who no doubt will be very pleased with the ships new look and increased range of facilities designed to give them the complete cruise experience. With her new role in offering fly cruises to the Mediterranean in 2014, it is good to know that the *Ventura* will be around for some time yet, so we can all appreciate why she is one of the most popular cruise ships ever to be designed exclusively for the British market.

The **Ventura** sails away from her home port as the Isle of Wight ferry, **Red Osprey**, approaches Town Quay. (Andrew Cooke)

The **Azura** looks splendid as she sails at speed in the sunshine of the
Mediterranean Sea. (P&O Cruises)

TECHNICAL SPECIFICATION FOR THE AZURA.

GENERAL INFORMATION

Builders: Fincantieri Cantieri Navali SpA, Monfalcone, Italy.
Yard Number: 6166
Contract Signed: 3rd January 2007
Contract Price: 480 Million Euros
Lead Design Architect: Giacomo Mortola
Date of Keel Laying Ceremony: 27th October 2008
Date of Float Up: 26th June 2009
Date of Delivery: 31st March 2010
Date of Naming Ceremony: 10th April 2010
Ships Godmother: Darcey Bussell
Date of Maiden Voyage: 12th April 2010
Call Sign: ZCEE2
IMO Number: 9424883
MMSI Number: 310610000
Classification: Lloyds Register +100A1 Passenger Ship.
Country of Registration: Bermuda
Passenger Capacity Double Occupancy: 3096
Maximum Passenger Capacity: 3597
Officers and Crew: 1226

TECHNICAL INFORMATION

Gross Tonnage: 115,055
Net Tonnage: 85,000
Maximum Displacement Tonnage: 52,723
Deadweight Tonnage : 8044
Length o.a: 289.60 Metres
Length p.p: Metres 242.20 Metres
Moulded Breadth: 36.0 Metres
Design Draught: 8.05 Metres
Maximum Draught 8.50 Metres
Maximum Air Draught: 67.40 Metres
Number of Decks: 18
Engines: 4 12V46C & 2 8L46C Wartsila Marine Diesel Engines
Total Engine Output: 67.2 Mega Watts
Shaft Output: 42 Mega Watts
Propellers: Wartsila 2 x 6 FP 5.6 Metre Blades
Thrusters: 3 x Bow @ 2200 KW each, 3 x Stern @ 1720KW each
Maximum Speed: 22.5 Knots
Service Speed: 21.5 knots
Fuel Consumption Average: 8.86 tonnes per hour.

LIFE SAVING EQUIPMENT

Tenders: 6
Motor Lifeboats: 18
Fast Rescue Boats: 2
Marine Escape Chutes: 4
Additional Life Rafts: 7

CABINS

2 Penthouse Suites
2 Family Suites
24 Suites
182 Deluxe Cabins
700 Twin Cabins with a balcony
207 Outside Cabins with a window
438 Inside Cabins
23 Disabled Cabins
18 Single Cabins

MAIN PUBLIC FACILITIES

Glass House Bar & Restaurant
Meridian Restaurant
Oriental Restaurant
Peninsular Restaurant
Poolside Grill
Seventeen Restaurant
Sindhu Restaurant
Venezia Restaurant
Verona Restaurant
Aqua Bar
Blue Note Bar
Breakers Bar
Brodies Bar & Casino
Coral Bar
Planet Bar
Terrace Bar
Java Coffee Bar
Malabar Show Lounge
Manhattan Show Lounge
Playhouse Theatre
Oasis Spa & Gymnasium
Four Swimming Pools
Retreat Wellbeing Area
Golf Nets
Sports Court
Sea Screen
Art Gallery
Photographer's Gallery
The Library
Children's Centre
Explorers Shore Excursion Desk
Atrium
Retail Area

AZURA

HAMILTON

*Another fine shot of the **Ventura** in Southampton Water shows her distinctly shaped stern as many passengers choose to enjoy the early evening sun. (Andrew Cooke)*

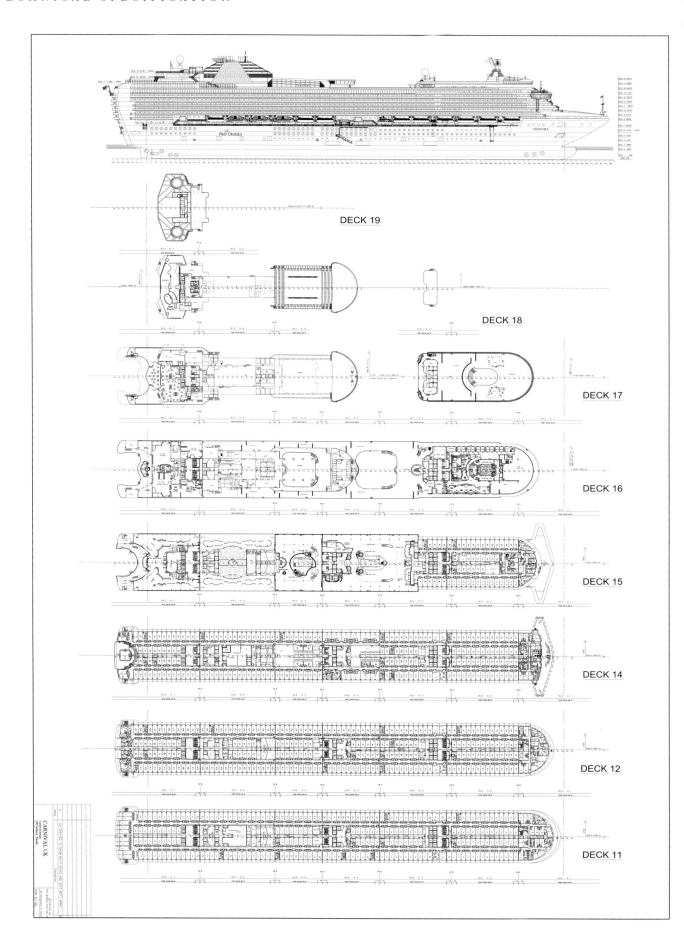

DECK 19

DECK 18

DECK 17

DECK 16

DECK 15

DECK 14

DECK 12

DECK 11

TECHNICAL SPECIFICATION FOR THE VENTURA.

GENERAL INFORMATION

Builders: Fincantieri Cantieri Navali SpA, Monfalcone, Italy.
Yard Number: 6132
Contract Signed: 23rd September 2004
Contract Price: 480 Million Euros
Lead Design Architect: Giacomo Mortola
Date of Keel Laying Ceremony: 29th August 2006
Date of Float Up: 08th June 2007
Date of Delivery: 29th March 2008
Date of Naming Ceremony: 16th April 2008
Ship's Godmother: Helen Mirren
Date of Maiden Voyage: 18th April 2008
Call Sign: ZCDT2
IMO Number: 9333175
MMSI Number: 310562000
Classification: Lloyds Register +100A1 Passenger Ship.
Country of Registration: Bermuda
Passenger Capacity Double Occupancy: 3086
Maximum Passenger Capacity: 3740
Officers and Crew: 1226

TECHNICAL INFORMATION

Gross Tonnage: 116,017
Net Tonnage: 85,255
Maximum Displacement Tonnage: 53,813
Deadweight Tonnage: 6750
Length o.a: 289.60 Metres
Length p.p: 242.20 Metres
Moulded Breadth: 36.00 Metres
Design Draught: 8.05 Metres
Maximum Draught: 8.50 Metres
Maximum Air Draft: 67.40 Metres
Number of Decks: 18
Engines: 4 X 12V46C & 2 X 8L46C Wartsila Marine Common Rail Diesel Engines
Total Engine Output: 67.2 Mega Watts
Shaft Output: 42 Mega Watts
Propellers: LIPS 2 x 5.6 Metre, FP 6 blades
Thrusters: 3 x Bow @ 2200 Kilowatts, 3 x Stern @ 1720Kw
Maximum Speed: 22.5 Knots
Service Speed: 21.5 knots
Fuel Consumption Average: 8.46 tonnes per hour.

LIFE SAVING EQUIPMENT

Tenders: 6
Motor Lifeboats: 18
Fast Rescue Boats: 2
Marine Escape Chutes: 4
Additional Life Rafts: 7

CABINS

2 Penthouse Suites
2 Family Suites
24 Suites
178 Deluxe Cabins
674 Twin Cabins with a balcony
232 Outside Cabins with a window
440 Inside Cabins
23 Disabled Cabins
18 Single Cabins

MAIN PUBLIC FACILITIES

Bay Tree Restaurant
Beach House Restaurant
Cinnamon Restaurant
East Restaurant
Frankie's Poolside Grill
Glass House Restaurant & Bar
Saffron Restaurant
Waterside Restaurant
White Room Restaurant
Beachcomber Bar
Breakers Bar
Exchange Bar & Casino
Laguna Poolside Bar
Metropolis Bar
Red Note Bar
Terrace Bar
Tazzine Coffee Bar
Havana Show Lounge
Tamarind Lounge
Arena Theatre
Oasis Spa & Gymnasium
Four Swimming Pools
Retreat Wellbeing Area
Golf Nets
Sports Court
Art Gallery
Photographer's Gallery
Chapter One Library
Children's Centre
Explorers Shore Excursion Desk
Atrium
Retail Area

Acknowledgements

The author would like to thank P&O Cruises Marketing Director, Christopher Edgington, for agreeing to write the Foreword for this book and also express his sincerest gratitude to David Strawford, the retired Fleet Services Director for Carnival UK, who has repeatedly given up his valuable time to help with many requests in compiling this book. A mention must also be made to Andrew Collier from the interior design company, SMC Design, who showed me around the Ventura whilst explaining the complexities of designing a modern cruise ship's interior. I would also like to thank Lynn Bianchi, Trevor Glass and Mike Jepson of P&O Cruises along with Emma Deighton, Richard Vie, Maurice Lowman and David Varty of Carnival UK for their assistance and help with my numerous requests for all sorts of information associated with this project. I must mention the crews of both the Azura and the Ventura, who were so very welcoming on every occasion that I visited them, both on busy turnaround days in Southampton and whilst the ships were at sea. They are an extremely hard-working group of talented people who are dedicated to providing their passengers with the best cruise experience possible and I hope I have done justice in conveying the extremely high standards they set for themselves.

From the Italian shipyard of Fincantieri, Stefano Giaconi deserves a mention for sharing with me his time and expertise and allowing access to the yard's photographic library and providing me with many images of the two ships under construction.

Finally, I would like to thank Rosalind Stimpson for editing the completed manuscript and Miles Cowsill of Ferry Publications who has done a magnificent job putting together yet another wonderful publication to add to his ever growing library of high-quality maritime books.